Anton Joly

Special thanks t

for proofing

STALINGRAD

BATTLE ATLAS

Part II

October 14 - November 18, 1942

One month of urban warfare operations

ISBN: 979-10-93222-05-9

To Soviet soldiers,

fallen defending their country

CONTENTS

INTRODUCTION

This second volume of the "Stalingrad Battle Atlas" series covers the period extending from October 14, the battle's doomsday on which the German might unleashed as never before, to the early hours of November 19, the day of the great Soviet counteroffensive, which was to become the beginning of the end for the invaders and ultimately for the third Reich itself.

Yet one month ago, on September 14, it seemed that Stalingrad's fate was sealed when German units reached the Volga soon after breaking into the city. The Red Army's resilience proved it wasn't so. Instead, the Wehrmacht eventually bogged down into vicious and durable urban warfare, where every inch of terrain was contested. This was an entirely new kind of conflict, which no army in the world had previously experienced, and where the traditional advantages of the German war machine were rubbed out.

There was no longer place for large-scale enveloping maneuvers led by strong tank forces. By now the armored vehicles operating among the ruins could only provide close support to the infantry without making use of their movement capacities, thus becoming particularly vulnerable targets. Nor could the air force deploy all its performance: since the opposing sides were entrenched unusually near to each other with positions often mingling together in an inextricable pattern, aircraft support to ground troops located on the frontline became ever more complicated and fruitless, though it still inflicted significant losses and impeded Soviet counterstrikes whenever units where acting on the open.

The contrast was great between the spectacular progress through vast expenses of the Ukraine in late spring and early summer, and the pitiful crawling through the ruined city in autumn. The advance, more and more slow since the Don, was no longer to be measured in kilometers. Here on the edge of the Volga, every building had to be taken one by one, whatever the cost.

In the wake of the very first days of street fighting in Stalingrad, German troops on the terrain were already convinced that the battle would be tough and long. In mid-October, after thirty days of intense and chaotic struggle, everyone in 6th Army and 4th Panzer Army, from the simple soldier to the Commander in chief, knew that any further progress would only become less significant and more toilsome than the previous one.

Yet as difficult as it was the advance continued.

In September as well as in October, all Soviet attempts to link up with Chuikov's besieged 62nd Army had been unsuccessful. However, they contributed to reduce German pressure on the city itself by forcing a considerable quantity of elite formations to defend 6th Army's and 4th Panzer Army's flanks, respectively along the Don facing north and around the salt lakes facing south and east.

The first major offensive period from September 13 to September 26 focused on the southern and central sectors of the city, extending roughly from the southern suburbs up to the borders of the workers' settlements flanking the industrial zone.

The second offensive period from September 27 to October 13 shifted the operations' gravity center northwards, with the workers' settlements and approaches of the giant factories as main theatres of operations.

Each time, despite a promising outset of their assault, the German attacking groups were eventually falling short of their ultimate objective, and saw their expectations frustrated by an amazing Soviet resistance capacity.

Now, after the equivalent of a full month of combats, the culminating point was about to be reached. Towards mid- October, after having completed a restructuration of his attacking forces, Paulus moved the most able formations into line, expecting the entire front to collapse in the northern sector of Stalingrad, then to finish off 62nd Army's truncated remnants with an enveloping maneuver along the Volga, as was his intent from the beginning.

By this time Stalingrad has essentially become a matter of prestige. Whereas for the Soviets it was indeed a question of survival in what was perceived as the ultimate battle, the last stand on the edge of the civilized world, the Germans were driven by even more symbolic reasons. Since their targets in the Caucasus could not have been achieved, the city on the Volga represented the only remaining prize still within their grasp which could give meaning to, and legitimate the whole summer campaign.

However, in Soviet plans, the city was not the real finality but part of a larger ensemble with more rational and ambitious objectives. Since late September the Soviet High Command had been considering the opportunity for a large counteroffensive on the distant flanks and rear of the German armies grouped in the Don-Volga region. Because the forces and material required for such an operation were considerable, time had become the key factor: it was necessary to freeze the situation which had developed during Army Group B's advance, to prevent the German command from reinforcing efficiently its overextended lines, while new resources could be gathered, equipped and deployed before breakthrough sectors. Initially planned for October, the offensive was gradually postponed until mid-November.

As determined through this larger strategic outlook, 62nd Army's role in Stalingrad was dreadfully basic, and even its own commander was not yet aware of the real issues at stake: to gain time while fixing 6th Army on the Volga. To hold on for one more month, to draw the most possible German strength into the maelstrom, to defend every possible spot, the last strips of ground, the last shore, at all cost.

Soviet Guardsmen in city center

CITY LANDMARKS

Actual landscape, autumn 1942

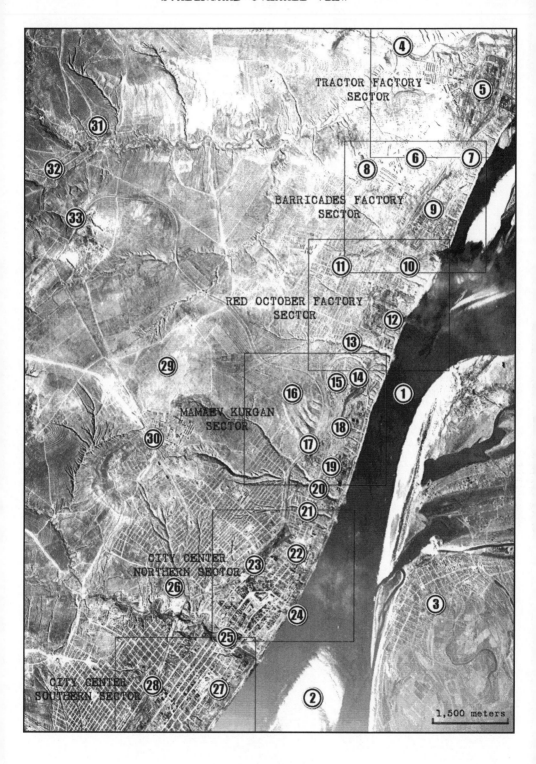

GENERAL LANDMARKS

1	Volga River
2	Golodny Island
3	Krasnaia Sloboda Village
4	Mechetka River
5	Dzerzhinsky Tractor Factory
6	Stadium
7	Brick Factory
8	Silicate Factory
9	Barrikady Gun Factory
10	Bread Factory
11	Workers Settlements
12	Red October Factory
13	Banny Ravine
14	Lazur Chemicals Factory
15	Meat Combine
16	Mamaev Kurgan
17	Metiz Factory
18	Tank Farm
19	Refinery
20	Dolgy Ravine
21	Krutoy Ravine
22	Ninth January Square
23	Central Station
24	Ferry Landing Stage
25	Tsaritsa River
26	Barracks
27	Grain Silo
28	Southern Station
29	Stalingradsky Airfield
30	Flying School Settlement
31	Gorodische Village
32	Aleksandrovka Village
33	Razgulaevka Village

1	Elshanka River	6	Canning Factory
2	Minina Suburb	7	Fire Department
3	Hospital	8	Depot
4	Southern Station	9	Tsaritsa River
5	Grain Elevator	10	Embankment Dam

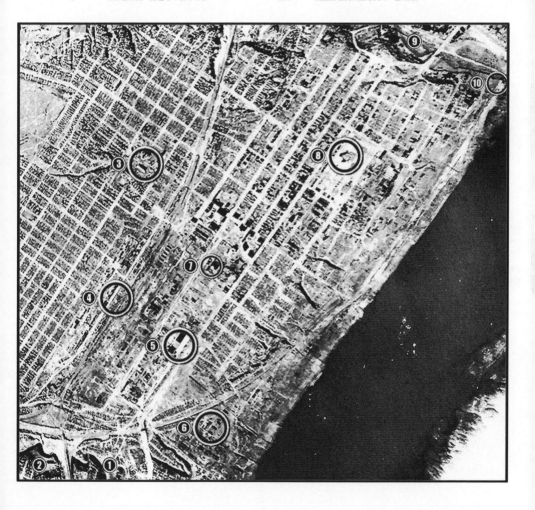

1	Tsaritsa River	11	Intourist Hotel
2	Tsaritsyn Bunker	12	Specialists Buildings
3	School	13	Gosbank
4	Warehouses	14	Brewery
5	Central Railway Station	15	NKVD Complex
6	Nail Factory	16	Ninth January Square
7	Komsomol Garden	17	Pavlov's House
8	Theater	18	Mill
9	Fallen Fighters Square	19	L-shaped House
10	Univermag Store	20	Krutoy Ravine

1	Dolgy Ravine	6	Water Cisterns
2	Metiz Factory	7	Meat Combine
3	Refinery	8	Lazur Chemicals Factory
4	Tank Farm	9	Oil Pipelines Main
5	Mamaev Kurgan	10	Banny Ravine

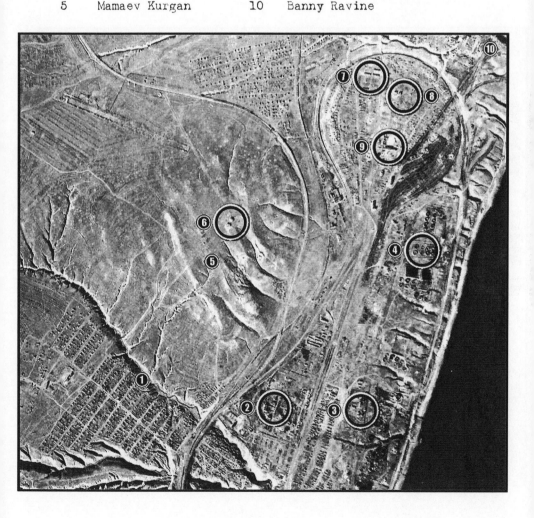

1   Banny Ravine
2   Oil Depot
3   Metallurgical Works "Red October" Plant
4   Workers' Settlements
5   Bread Factory

1   Bread Factory
2   Oil Depot
3   Gun Factory "Barricades" Complex
4   Workers' Settlements
5   Silicate Factory
6   Six-sided block and Stadium
7   Brick Factory

1   Brick Factory
2   Workers' Settlements
3   Dzerzhinsky Tractor Factory
4   Oil Depot
5   Zhitomirsk Ravine
6   Mechetka River

14-15 October

16-19 October

22-29 October

11-18 November

20,21,26,27,28 October
30 October - 06 November

23-25 October
10 November

800 meters

14-15 October
Tractor Factory Sector

16-19 October
Barricades Factory Outskirts

20-21 October
Barricades and Red October Factories

22 October
Barricades Factory

23-25 October
Red October Factory

26-28 October
Barricades and Red October Factories

29 October
Barricades Factory

30 October – 03 November
Barricades and Red October Factories

10 November
Red October Factory

11-18 November
Barricades Factory

SOVIET UNIT KEY

Front	XXXXX ⊠
	STALINGRAD FRONT
Combined Army	XXXX 21 ⊠
Tank Army	XXXX 5 ⬭
Rifle Corps	XXX 8 ⊠
Mechanized Corps	XXX 4 ⊠
Tank Corps	XXX 1 ⬭
Cavalry Corps	XXX 8 ⊠
Rifle Division	XX 196 ⊠
Motorized Rifle Division	XX 3 ⊠
Cavalry Division	XX 81 ⬭
Rifle Brigade	X 149 ⊠
Motorized Rifle Brigade	X 2 ⊠
Tank Brigade	X 6 ⬭
Guards formation	XX 50 ⊠

Army Group

XXXXX

ARMY GROUP B

Field Army

6 XXXX

Panzer Army

4 XXXX

Army Corps

8 XXX

Panzer Corps

48 XXX

Infantry Division

100 XX

Motorized Infantry Division

3 XX

Panzer Division

14 XX

Cavalry Division

1 XX

Romanian formation

5 XX

Soviet submachine gunner covering the advance of his fellow soldiers

ONE MONTH OF URBAN WARFARE

Operations in the city from October 14 to November 18, 1942

THE CLOUDS GATHER

Towards mid-October the situation in the city is contrasted between north and south.

German troops hold the southern districts and suburbs of the city, most of the center and the greater part of Mamaev Kurgan. They are also well advanced into the industrial zone, controlling almost all of the worker settlements, and already standing not very far from the factories themselves. The omnipresent formation there is Seydlitz's 51st Army Corps, which led the advance in the city since the beginning of the assault thirty days ago.

Soviet troops hold a tiny strip of land in city center, the refinery section and part of Mamaev Kurgan eastern slope, with respectively Rodimtsev's 13th Guards Division and Batiuk's 284th Division. The bulk of 62nd Army is concentrated north of these positions and deployed around the three imposing factory complexes and their adjacent streets, with territory widening when going northwards. At the northernmost part of the front, operational Group Gorokhov is holding an even larger salient extending from beyond the Mechetka River up to the village of Elshanka, where it faces units of Hube's 14th Panzer Corps and the German land corridor.

In these northern areas Chuikov's army is still defending a territory extending up to 1,500 meters from the Volga, while in the southern part of the city this distance can be down ten times, reaching no more than 150 meters from the river in some sectors.

During the lull in the fighting between October 6 and October 13, both sides proceeded to a regrouping of their forces. While the front remained relatively quiet in the city center all the way up to Mamaev Kurgan, with Soviet and German factions by now altogether entrenched within their respective positions, all new troops were directed to the industrial district, especially in front of the Barricades (Баррикады) and Tractor (Тракторный) factories where the offensive operations were to take place.

Ruins in city center

Hierarchical structure for armies on the Don and Volga

OBERKOMMANDO DES HEERES

CHIEF OF GENERAL STAFF
Kurt Zeitzler

COMMANDER IN CHIEF
Adolf Hitler

CHIEF OF OPERATIONS
Adolf Heusinger

ARMY GROUP B

CHIEF OF STAFF
Georg von Sodenstern

COMMANDER
Maximilian von Weichs

CHIEF OF OPERATIONS
August Winter

HUNGARIAN 2ND ARMY
Gusztav Jany

ITALIAN 8TH ARMY
Italo Gariboldi

ROMANIAN 3RD ARMY
Petre Dumitrescu

6TH ARMY
Friedrich Paulus

4TH PANZER ARMY
Hermann Hoth

Hierarchical structure for armies on the Don and Volga

STAVKA VERKHOVNOVO GLAVNOKOMANDOVANIA

DEPUTY COMMANDER
Georgy Zhukov

SUPREME COMMANDER
Iosif Stalin

CHIEF OF GENERAL STAFF
Aleksandr Vasilevsky

DON FRONT

CHIEF OF STAFF
Mikhail Malinin

COMMANDER
Konstantin Rokossovsky

POLITICAL OFFICER
Aleksey Kirichenko

21ST ARMY
Ivan Chistiakov

24TH ARMY
Ivan Galanin

4TH TANK ARMY
Vasily Kriuchenkin

66TH ARMY
Aleksey Zhadov

VOLGA FLOTILLA
Dmitry Rogache

STALINGRAD FRONT

CHIEF OF STAFF
Ivan Varennikov

COMMANDER
Andrey Eremenko

POLITICAL OFFICER
Nikita Khruschev

62ND ARMY
Vasily Chuikov

64RD ARMY
Mikhail Shumilov

57TH ARMY
Fedor Tolbukhin

51st ARMY
Nikolay Trufanov

28TH ARMY
Vasily Gerasimer

6ᵀᴴ ARMY

CHIEF OF STAFF
Arthur Schmidt

COMMANDER
Friedrich Paulus

CHIEF OF OPERATIONS
Wilhelm Adam

14ᵀᴴ PANZER CORPS

COMMANDER
Hans-Valentin Hube

60ᵀᴴ MOTORIZED DIVISION
Otto Kohlermann

3ᴿᴰ MOTORIZED DIVISION
Helmuth Schlömer

16ᵀᴴ PANZER DIVISION
Günther Angern

51ˢᵀ ARMY CORPS

COMMANDER
Walther von Seydlitz-Kurzbach

94ᵀᴴ INFANTRY DIVISION
Georg Pfeiffer

389ᵀᴴ INFANTRY DIVISION
Erwin Jänecke

305ᵀᴴ INFANTRY DIVISION
Kurt Oppenländer

14ᵀᴴ PANZER DIVISION
Ferdinand Heim

24ᵀᴴ PANZER DIVISION
Arno von Lenski

100ᵀᴴ JAGER DIVISION
Werner Sanne

295ᵀᴴ INFANTRY DIVISION
Rolf Wuthmann

48ᵀᴴ PANZER CORPS

COMMANDER
Werner Kempf

71ˢᵀ INFANTRY DIVISION
Alexander von Hartmann

29ᵀᴴ MOTORIZED DIVISION
Hans-Georg Leyser

62ⁿᵈ ARMY

CHIEF OF STAFF
Nikolay Krylov

COMMANDER
Vasily Chuikov

POLITICAL OFFICER
Kuzma Gurov

L GROUP GOROKHOV

124ᵀᴴ RIFLE BRIGADE
Sergey Gorokhov

149ᵀᴴ RIFLE BRIGADE
Vasily Bolvinov

L ARMY UNITS

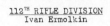

112ᵀᴴ RIFLE DIVISION
Ivan Ermolkin

84ᵀᴴ TANK BRIGADE
Danil Bely

37ᵀᴴ GRD RIFLE DIVISION
Victor Zholudev

95ᵀᴴ RIFLE DIVISION
Vasily Gorishny

308ᵀᴴ RIFLE DIVISION
Leonty Gurtiev

193ᴿᴰ RIFLE DIVISIO
Fedor Smekhotvoro

39ᵀᴴ GRD RIFLE DIVISION
Stepan Guriev

284ᵀᴴ RIFLE DIVISION
Nikolay Batiuk

13ᵀᴴ GRD RIFLE DIVIS
Aleksandr Rodimtse

Approximate unit strength of units attacking the city or vicinity, from north to south

60th Motorized Infantry Division (30 tanks)	8,000
3rd Motorized Infantry Division (30 tanks)	5,500
16th Panzer Division (50 tanks)	7,500
94th Infantry Division	4,500
14th Panzer Corps total	<u>25,500</u>
Part of which actually facing Stalingrad (20 tanks)	10,000
389th Infantry Division	3,500
305th Infantry Division	13,000
14th Panzer Division (50 tanks)	9,500
24th Panzer Division (30 tanks)	3,000
100th Jäger Division	5,000
295th Infantry Division	6,500
51st Army Corps total (80 tanks, 20 assault guns)	40,500
71st Infantry Division	8,500
48th Panzer Corps total	8,500
Total German 6th Army forces (120 tanks and AG)	59,000

Approximate unit strength of units defending the city or vicinity, from north to south

124th Rifle Brigade	3,500
149th Rifle Brigade	2,500
Group Gorokhov total	**6,000**
112th Rifle Division	2,000
37th Guards Rifle Division	4,500
84th Tank Brigade (20 tanks)	500
95th Rifle Division	2,500
308th Rifle Division	2,500
193th Rifle Division	3,500
39th Guards Rifle Division	5,000
284th Rifle Division	5,500
13th Guards Rifle Division	6,000
Other Army-related formations and services (20 tanks)	4,000
Total Soviet 62nd Army forces (40 tanks)	**42,000**

THE STORM UNLEASHES

On October 14, 1942, while hundreds of tons of steel where hurled against Soviet defenders in what was considered as the German D-day for Stalingrad, Hitler issued the winter standby directive to his troops on the eastern front. It read: "This year's summer and fall campaign, excepting the operations currently under way and several local offensives still contemplated, has been concluded." As for the "operations currently under way" 6th Army was ordered not only to continue, but also to strengthen its offensive.

Although badly depleted for the most part, the divisions mustered by both sides in the industrial district of the city still embodied a considerable fighting potential. With regard to density, seldom in the history of wars such a small territory was contested by such a quantity of manpower, artillery and aircraft.

It can be assumed that on the eve of the new offensive in the northern part of Stalingrad, German assault groups were numbering an aggregated total of about 40,000 men as opposed to about 20,000 Soviet defenders.

Since 6th Army's engineering stations were able repair a great number of vehicles, about 120 tanks and assault guns were available for the new German offensive. Soviet armored forces, representing less than 40 tanks, were essentially reduced to 84th Tank Brigade, spared because recently arrived on the battlefield, and 1st Special Tank Brigade, consisting of the local production from the Tractor Factory itself.

The factory chains continued running whenever possible until the last moment. As soon as a machine was ready to roll from the assembly line, the workers who built or repaired it became soldiers, driving their half-finished tank into the battle, which was raging nearer each day and was now almost right in front of them.

Artillery and mortar shelling begins before dawn. As aviation joins in, distinct explosions can no longer be heard, mixing into an earthquake. Whereas 389th Division attacks along the Mechetka River, the main assault group (14th Panzer and 305th Infantry Divisions) attacks towards the Tractor Factory. Another assault group led by 24th Panzer Division attacks along the Zhitomirsk Ravine south of the giant plant.

By noon, several Soviet units are crushed by the German onslaught and the whole 416th [1], 109th [2] and 117th [3] Regiments of 37th Guards Rifle Division are surrounded.

In the afternoon, the main German assault group [1] breaks into the southern part of the Tractor Factory. At midnight, most of the factory is invested and some detachments even reach the Volga behind, but savage fighting continues inside the ruined workshops and the panzer grenadiers reverse momentarily in order to let the artillery shell at will the northern section of the complex [2]. Despite stubborn Soviet resistance, the second assault group [3] also makes good progress, closing in on the Brick Factory and 62nd Army's HQ.

Other sectors: North of the Mechetka River 14th Panzer Corps gains ground on Group Gorokhov.

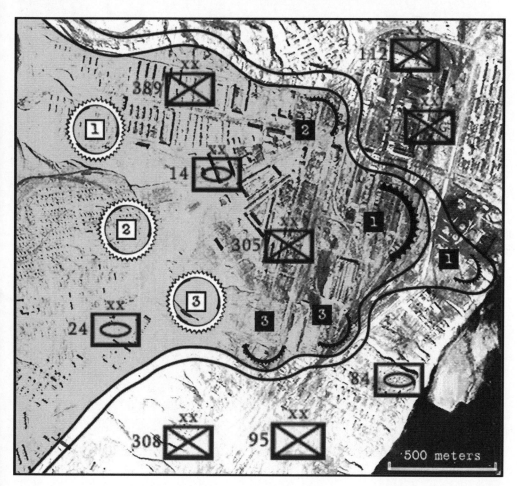

The northernmost part of the Tractor Factory

★ *Major-General N.I. Krylov, 62ⁿᵈ Army Chief of Staff:*

On the night of October 14 the enemy was unusually quiet. Scarce machine-gun fire could be heard from the frontline. This uncommon silence did not predict anything good. At 5:30 in the morning, it was broken by the roar of engines and explosions [...] The shallow tunnel that housed our HQ staggered as from an earthquake. At its entrance, the continuous howl from bombs and shells prevented hearing one's voice [...] For a time the telephone partly operated. Then our units could be reached only by radio: some directly, others through more powerful transmitters from over the Volga. There was no time for encryption, the broadcasts were in plain text [...] Our staff members were doing their job with an outward calm, although everyone was aware that a decisive day had come for Stalingrad [...] [2]

★ *Lieutenant-General V.I. Chuikov, 62ⁿᵈ Army Commander*

That day we did not see the sun, save for a brown stain occasionally peeking through gaps in clouds of smoke [...] Under cover of a hurricane of fire along a 6 km-front, three infantry and two armored divisions stormed our formations, greatly weakened by the previous fights [...] Our dugout was shaking feverishly, the earth rang, sand was falling from the ceiling [...] What I saw and heard outside is hard to describe. Dive bombers engines roared, bombs howled, everything around was growling, moaning and exploding [...] By 15:00 enemy armored units penetrated deep into our positions. They reached the outskirts of the Tractor and Barricades factories. Our garrisons were scattered and surrounded but still fought, restraining the German onslaught [...] Yet enemy tanks managed to break through and arrived within 300 meters of the Army's command post. The HQ's guard company went into the fight [...] Detachments of worker militia were defending the factories along with regular army troops, fighting to the last bullet [...] Separate enemy groups reached the banks of the Volga behind the Tractor Plant. 62ⁿᵈ Army was split up once again.[1]

German progression through the Tractor Plant continues all night and morning, impeded by rearguard actions from separate groups inside the factory halls [1]. By the afternoon, Soviet defenses in and around the complex are crushed altogether and the Volga is reached along the whole sector [1].

With the entire complex occupied, German troops now turn towards the Barricades Factory [2], directly threatening Chuikov's command post defended by an emergency force including all HQ guard.

Other sectors: North of the Mechetka River 16th Panzer, 94th and 389th Infantry Divisions join for a combined attack against Group Gorokhov north of the factory. German troops reach the landing stage at the Mechetka river's mouth, cuting off 124th and 149th brigades from the bulk of 62nd Army.

German casualties for the last two days: around 1,000 men and 30 tanks.
Soviet casualties for the last two days: around 10,000 men. 3,700 wounded are ferried across the Volga.

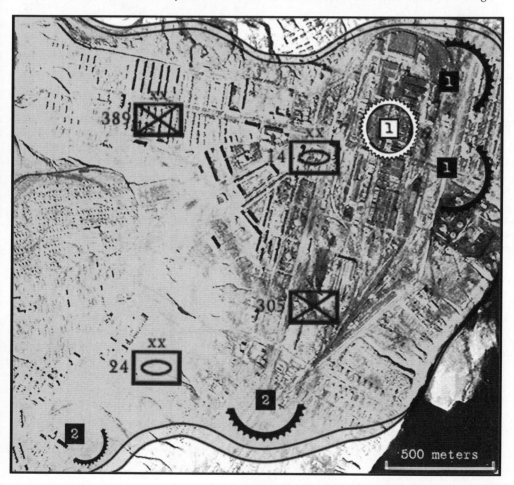

Amid the chaos of metal in factory halls

★ *Major-General N.I. Krylov, 62ⁿᵈ Army Chief of Staff:*

On the morning of the 15th all started over again: a violent bombing barrage across our defenses, infantry and tank attacks... The enemy, which had not yet entirely conquered the Tractor Factory and was still fighting within, was in a hurry to extend yesterday's breakthrough to the plant northward and southward along the Volga [...] German machine gunners appeared 500 meters from the Army's command post and the HQ security was called in [...] Despite the complex situation of our Army's main forces, our anxiety about Group Gorokhov did not lessen. The enemy assaulted it from three sides: 94th Division attacked from the factory district, 389th Division advanced from the west along the Mechetka river, 16th Panzer came down from the north towards the village of Rynok. The only help we could provide to the surrounded brigades was artillery fire. But Gorokhov's reports confirmed: the Northern Group was holding firm.[2]

★ *Lieutenant-General V.I. Chuikov, 62ⁿᵈ Army Commander*

The devastating onslaught was going on. We were aware of the enemy's preparations for a major attack with superior forces, but frankly, we did not anticipate such a mighty strike. We realized that the decisive battle had come, and that if we can survive it, the Germans were unlikely to muster such powerful forces again. We knew that this was the ultimate ordeal, for us and for the enemy [...] The divisions of Ermolkin, Zholudev and the right flank of Gurtiev were fighting in encirclement [...] Reports were conflicting and their refining was ever more difficult. Command and observation posts of regiments and divisions were smashed out by shells and bombs. Many commanders perished. There were 30 casualties at the sole Army HQ [...] By midnight October 15 it appeared that the enemy completely surrounded the Tractor Plant and was fighting inside its workshops.[1]

Colonel Liudnikov's 138th Rifle Divison's 650th Regiment (about 2,500 men) is ferried overnight and directed towards the Barricades Factory [1] yet it lacks the time to deploy before the German assault.

After regrouping 51st Corps renew the onslaught to the Barricades Factory. Attacking its northwestern outskirts, 36th Panzer Regiment succeeds in driving back 95th Division's depleted forces before 138th Division could entrench in its designated forward positions. The advanced detachments of 103rd and 576th Regiments eventually seize a portion of the factory [1]. Dug-in Soviet tanks from 84th Brigade, backed up by appropriate Katyusha rocket salvoes, impede the German advance to the north of the factory [2]. After hours of intense fire exchange, about 15 vehicles end up destroyed on each side.

Other sectors: Group Gorokhov is now isolated north of the Mechetka River. After three days of ruthless fighting, the overall Soviet defensive strength is down by 50%. 37th Guards, 112th Division, 42nd and 92nd Brigades are virtually wiped out, while 95th Divisions sustained 80% losses.

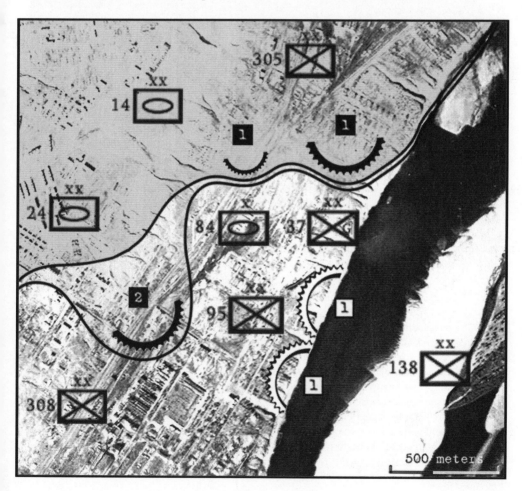

★ *Major-General N.I. Krylov, 62ⁿᵈ Army Chief of Staff:*

We owe to our tank crews to have kept most of our lines in the central sector on October 16. The "armored force" of our army consisted of Colonel Bely's brigade, which arrived two weeks ago. The tanks were to be used on fixed positions only. If at first we had been disappointed with these restrictions, now it was time to appreciate them [...] Our anti-tank defenses were arranged along the only supposed way for our opponent to move its tanks southward in this sector. There we decided to dig into the ground some T-34, up to the tower, carefully disguised. The enemy did not detect their presence, so they could suddenly open a direct fire on German tanks from a distance of 100-200 meters. The heading machines were quickly destroyed, blocking the way for the rest. Behind the tanks followed infantry on trucks: apparently the enemy has decided that he could sweep our defense on the run [...] The advance stalled. Some surviving tanks began to back away. Then our artillery from over the Volga opened fire upon the accumulation of enemy manpower and equipment. It took some time for German headquarters to get a clear picture of the situation, the operation was not called off and new units continued to come up. Our artillery was crushing them down. After Pozharsky [62ⁿᵈ Army's Artillery commander] added to that a Katyusha salvo, the Germans began to panic [...] The main approaches of the Barricades Factory were thus protected.[2]

✚ *Oberkommando des Heeres information report for 16.10.1942:*

In Stalingrad infantry and tank units in close cooperation with continuously attacking aircraft continued to advance despite the desperate resistance of the enemy, destroyed a large number of fortifications and dug-in tanks, then broke into the "Red Barricade" gun factory. As a result of the strike in the northern direction, enemy troops northwest of the city were cut off from their supply lines and are expected to be soon destroyed.[3]

At Stalin's request, Eremenko crosses the Volga to visit 62nd Army's HQ on the night of October 17 to assess the situation on the terrain. Chuikov is also advised to move his HQ further south.

The rest of 138th Division (344th and 768th Regiments) cross the Volga, manning positions in the Barricades Factory and beyond [1], backed by the last forces of 37th Guards Division's 118th Regiment.

In the wake of 24th Panzer Division's advance [1], 308th Rifle Division's 339th [2] and 347th [3] Regiments are encircled near the factory's western side, their men keeping on fighting individually or in small groups for another three days. The remainder of Gurtiev's troops joins Liudnikov's inside the complex, whereas the remnants of 95th Division redeploy around the Bread Factory.

Other sectors: Greatly outnumbered by 14th Panzer Corps, Group Gorokhov continues to fight in encirclement north of the Mechetka River. The losses are considerable for both sides.

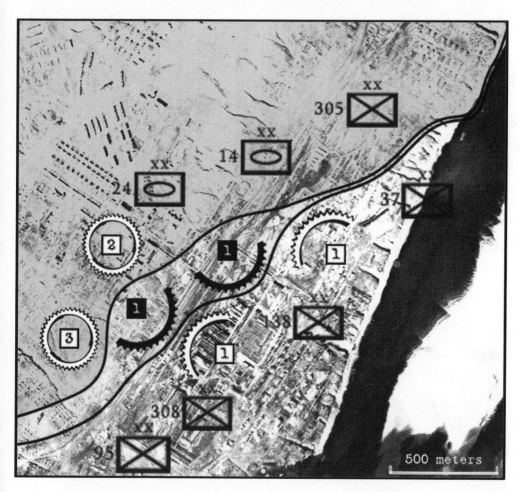

At the Stalingrad Front headquarters, Khruschev (left) and Eremenko (right)

★ *Lieutenant-General V.I. Chuikov, 62nd Army Commander*

On the night of October 17, I was informed that we should expect the Front Commander, Colonel-General Eremenko. Gurov and I went to the dock to meet them. German six-barrel mortars were firing incessantly on the Volga. Hundreds of wounded crawled towards the ferry's pier. Our HQ itself presented a bleak picture. The shelters had turned into craters, wooden beams sticking out of the ground [...] That night the rest of 138th Division arrived at last. We immediately directed it toward the Barricades Factory.[1]

★ *Major-General N.I. Krylov, 62nd Army Chief of Staff:*

Colonel General Eremenko arrived before our Commander had returned. I had to meet the boss myself. "I came to see if you are still alive here" said the Front Commander entering the tunnel. Candidly, he added: "Comrade Stalin himself ordered to visit you and to report what's going on here" [...] We dealt especially with Gurtiev's 308th Division, which fought valiantly, but badly needed replenishment [...] At midnight a tall colonel with dark eyebrows came in. It was 138th Division's Commander. After listening to his report, Eremenko stressed that there was no possible retreat. "Is it clear to you?" he asked. "Clear" said Liudnikov.[2]

★ *Colonel L.N. Gurtiev, 308th Division Commander:*

In the most difficult moments, when it seemed that there was no more way out [of semi-encirclement on the Barricades Factory's outskirts], we all took our guns and made ready to fight to the end. No one even thought of getting away. If we looked towards the Volga, it was only because of our longing for supplies and reinforcements...[4]

Paulus and Seydlitz regroup their forces around the Barricades Factory to proceed with its storming. However, these succeed only in grasping some dozens meters more in the plant's western part [1] encountering ferocious resistance and counterattacks in each workshop, hall and recess where 138th and 308th Divisions have tightened their defenses.

The attempt to overrun the Soviet lines with an advance from the vicinity of the Brick Factory [2] is not more successful, each meter of terrain contested by 650th Regiment backed by the last remaining soldiers from 118th Guards Regiment.

62nd Army HQ's location [1] is moved again, southwards on the Volga bank between Mamaev Kurgan and the Red October Factory, where it will remain until the end of the Stalingrad operations.

Other sectors: In other sectors the situation remains unchanged.

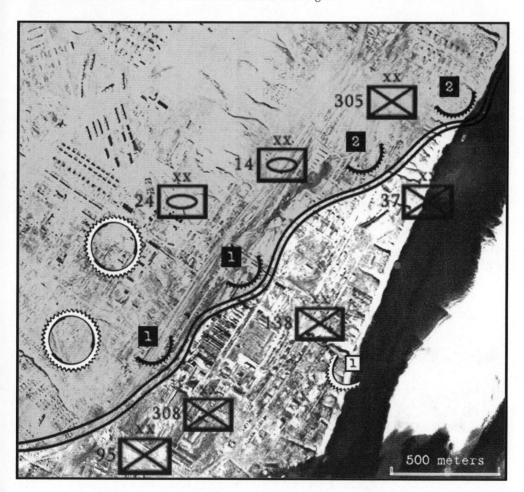

Soviet riflemen in faction in the northern sector of the front

★ *V.S. Grossman, war press correspondent:*

The Germans launched a decisive assault on the Barricades Factory, preceding it with an awesome bombardment. Aviation, heavy mortars and artillery worked for eighty consecutive hours. Three days and three nights turned into a chaos of smoke, fire and thunder. The fizz of bombs, the squeaking roar of sextuple mortars, the rumble of heavy shells, the screeching sirens where enough to deafen people, yet they were only a prelude to the blasts. Ragged flames from explosions blazed, the howling of tortured metal drilled the space. So it was during eighty hours. Then appeared tanks and infantry. The Germans managed to break into the factory, their tanks roared along the workshops, they ripped up our defenses, cutting off command posts from the troops. It seemed that [308th] division, deprived of management, would lose the ability to resist [...] But something formidable happened: each trench, each dugout, every foxhole and fortified ruins of houses turned into a fortress with its own command system, with its own communications. Sergeants and privates became commanders, skillfully and wisely repelling attacks. And in this bitter hour, commanders and staff officers turned their headquarters into defense positions and themselves into ordinary soldiers, fighting off enemy attacks. The regimental Commander himself was firing a mortar.[5]

★ *62nd Army report to the STAVKA for 18.10.1942:*

At 10:45 October 18 the enemy resumed the offensive on the "Barricades" factory from the north with at least one infantry regiment with 30 tanks, and with at least one infantry regiment from the west. After heavy fighting the enemy managed to break through to the southern edge of the "Barricades" Factory at the end of the day. Our troops continued to hold the factory. In this battle, 18 enemy tanks were destroyed.[3]

Whereas the German assault groups are already showing signs of weakening, heavy rains restrict Luftwaffe support. Yet the assault on the Barricades Factory carries on.

In the northern halls, Oppenländer's 576th and 578th Regiments are checked by Liudnikov's 344th and 768th Regiments. Sustaining severe losses, the attack is called off soon after it began. Then 138th Division counterattacks and regains most of the factory from 305th Division [1].

On the other side 103rd Panzer Regiment succeeds in entering the southwestern part of the complex [1].

Other sectors: In other sectors the situation remains unchanged.

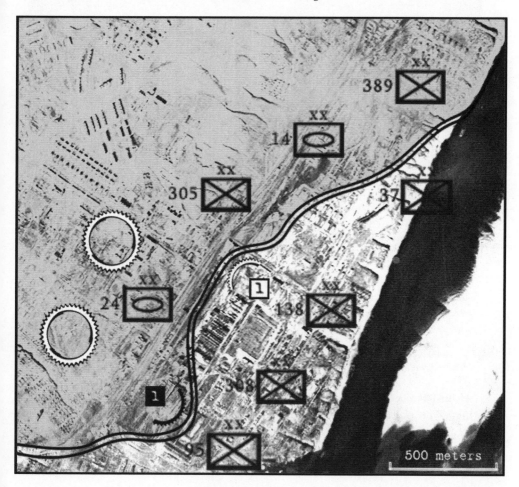

German infantry in a ruined workshop

★ *V.S. Grossman, war press correspondent:*

This unprecedentedly fierce battle lasted for several days on. It was no longer for separate houses and shops, it was for every single stair, for a corner in a narrow passage, for a separate machine-tool, for the span between machines, for a pipe section. In this battle no one turned back. And if the Germans occupied any location, it meant that there was no longer any living Red Army soldier. It was as though the fallen transferred their strength to the survivors, and there were moments when ten men successfully held a battalion-sized sector. Many times the factory shops passed from the Siberians to the Germans before being seized again by the Siberians. In this battle, the Germans occupied several halls and workshops. In this battle, the German attack reached its maximum degree of tension. It was their highest strike potential. Like lifting an excessive burden, they tore some internal springs activating their ram. The German pressure curve then began to fall. The Siberians withstood this superhuman tension. Two thousand tons of scrapped metal from tanks lay down in front of the factory. Thousands of tons of bombs and shells were dropped on the factory yard, on the workshops, but the men of 308th Division stood the strain. They did not left this last boundary, they never looked back, knowing that behind them was the Volga, whereas before them lied the whole country's fate.[5]

✚ *Oberkommando des Heeres information report for 19.10.1942:*

The Wehrmacht units advancing in Stalingrad crushed the fiercely defending enemy, stormed the shops of the "Red Barricade" arms factory, then after reflecting powerful counterattacks in bloody battles, expelled the Soviets out of the surrounding blocks.[3]

47

The bad weather persisting, 6th Army reorganizes for upcoming operations while 62nd Army consolidates its positions. After a week of intense fighting, Germans troops engaged in the industrial sector have lost 30% of their personal strength, while tank losses reach as far as 70%.

Soviet casualties are even more appalling. Almost reduced to their sole headquarters, 37th, 95th and 112th Divisions are sent back across the Volga. Their few remaining forces pass under the control of 138th and 193rd Divisions. Yet despite increasing erosion the lines continue to hold firm, and it is now clear that the offensive has spent itself again.

Schwerin's 79th Infantry Division, coming from the Don, joins 51st Army Corps assault groups in the city. For the moment only 208th [1] and 212th [2] Regiments are committed, 226th Regiment is yet to come.

Other sectors: In other sectors the situation remains unchanged.

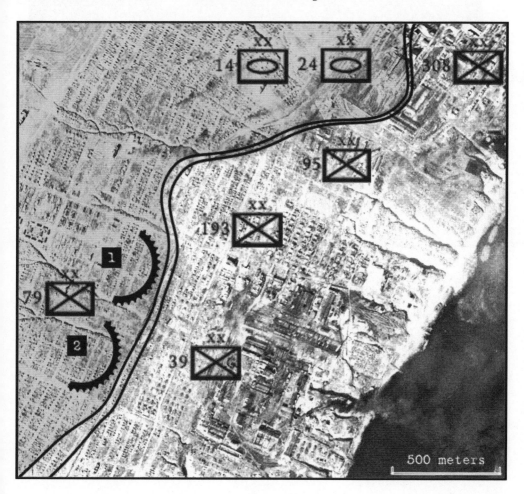

German infantry in front of the Red October Factory

★ *Soviet national newspaper Pravda, 20.10.1942:*

In Stalingrad Soviet troops fought stubborn defensive battles. The fighting goes on day and night. Calling in reserves, the Germans launched another offensive in the northern part of the city. Enemy infantry supported by 40 tanks attacked our strong points in the worker villages' area. After a fierce battle our forces threw the Germans back to their original positions, causing them heavy losses. After some time, the Germans brought up a few dozen tanks and renewed their offensive. The second nazi attack was fended off like the first. The enemy rolled back, losing a large number of tanks and troops. By the end of the day the battle still raged on the same frontline. Our soldiers are fighting with tenacity and perseverance. Infantrymen, artillerymen, tankmen are grinding down enemy materiel and manpower despite fierce bombardments. Within one day our troops wrecked a large number of German tanks. Soviet pilots, successfully covering the infantry formations, shot down many enemy aircraft. Airman Lavrenenko fought with several German fighters. His plane was damaged, and Lavrenenko was wounded. Despite this, he destroyed a Messerschmitt-109 in a frontal attack then returned safely to his base. Fighter pilots led by Major Chuykin met with a large group of aircraft. In the ensuing battle, our fighters shot down 8 of them.[5]

✚ *Wehrmacht GHQ information report for 20.10.1942:*

On the northern outskirts of Stalingrad, German troops occupied several more buildings. The fights for liberation from the enemy of the "Red Barricade" munitions factory area are still going on. Aviation tactical support inflicted major damage to heavily fortified strongholds in the "Red October" factory. On the lower reaches of the Volga, our bombers destroyed several transport convoys, one barge, and six aircraft on an airfield.[3]

6ᵀᴴ ARMY

CHIEF OF STAFF
Arthur Schmidt

COMMANDER
Friedrich Paulus

CHIEF OF OPERATIONS
Wilhelm Adam

L 14ᵀᴴ PANZER CORPS

COMMANDER
Hans-Valentin Hube

60ᵀᴴ MOTORIZED DIVISION
Otto Kohlermann

3ᴿᴰ MOTORIZED DIVISION
Helmuth Schlömer

16ᵀᴴ PANZER DIVISION
Günther Angern

L 51ˢᵀ ARMY CORPS

COMMANDER
Walther von Seydlitz-Kurzbach

94ᵀᴴ INFANTRY DIVISION
Georg Pfeiffer

389ᵀᴴ INFANTRY DIVISION
Erwin Jänecke

24ᵀᴴ PANZER DIVISION
Arno von Lenski

305ᵀᴴ INFANTRY DIVISION
Kurt Oppenländer

14ᵀᴴ PANZER DIVISION
Ferdinand Heim

79ᵀᴴ INFANTRY DIVISION
Richard von Schwerin

100ᵀᴴ JAGER DIVISION
Werner Sanne

L 48ᵀᴴ PANZER CORPS

COMMANDER
Werner Kempf

295ᵀᴴ INFANTRY DIVISION
Rolf Wuthmann

71ˢᵀ INFANTRY DIVISION
Alexander von Hartmann

29ᵀᴴ MOTORIZED DIVISION
Hans-Georg Leyser

------------------------------   62nd ARMY   ------------------------------

CHIEF OF STAFF
Nikolay Krylov

COMMANDER
Vasily Chuikov

POLITICAL OFFICER
Kuzma Gurov

L GROUP GOROKHOV ------------------------------

124TH RIFLE BRIGADE
Sergey Gorokhov

149TH RIFLE BRIGADE
Vasily Bolvinov

L ARMY UNITS ----- ------------------------------

138TH RIFLE DIVISION
Ivan Liudnikov

308TH RIFLE DIVISION
Leonty Gurtiev

193RD RIFLE DIVISION
Fedor Smekhotvorov

39TH GRD RIFLE DIVISION
Stepan Guriev

284TH RIFLE DIVISION
Nikolay Batiuk

13TH GRD RIFLE DIVISION
Aleksandr Rodimtsev

Approximate unit strength of units attacking the city or vicinity, from north to south

60th Motorized Infantry Division (30 tanks)	9,500
3rd Motorized Infantry Division (30 tanks)	8,000
16th Panzer Division (50 tanks)	6,000
94th Infantry Division	4,500
14th Panzer Corps total	28,000
Part of which actually facing Stalingrad (20 tanks)	11,000
389th Infantry Division	4,000
24th Panzer Division (10 tanks)	3,000
305th Infantry Division	10,000
14th Panzer Division (25 tanks)	7,000
79th Infantry Division	9,000
100th Jäger Division	7,000
295th Infantry Division	6,500
51st Army Corps total (35 tanks, 15 assault guns)	46,500
71st Infantry Division	7,500
48th Panzer Corps total	8,500
Total German 6th Army forces (70 tanks and AG)	66,000

Approximate unit strength of units defending the city or vicinity, from north to south

124th Rifle Brigade	3,000
149th Rifle Brigade	2,000
Group Gorokhov total	**5,000**
138th Rifle Division	2,500
308th Rifle Division	2,000
193th Rifle Division	3,500
39th Guards Rifle Division	4,500
284th Rifle Division	5,000
13th Guards Rifle Division	6,000
Other Army-related formations and services	2,000
Total Soviet 62nd Army forces (10 tanks)	**30,500**

By devising their third and most powerful offensive in the city, Army Group B and 6th Army's Command were clearly determined to "finish off" the defenders of Stalingrad. Indeed the fighting on October 14 and 15 was described as fantastic.

The means deployed for German ground troops support were impressive with regard to the surface to be covered. More than one thousand aircraft, all Luftwaffe forces available in the region, flew multiple sorties all day long. Artillery and mortars concentrated their shelling on just a few square miles for more than two hours before the reinforced infantry and tanks units moved on.

On Soviet side, artillery fire intensified from the eastern bank of the Volga, but the VVS could not help Chuikov's troops in the city because Khriukin's 8th Air Army's airfields were completely blocked by swarms of German fighters from Richthofen's 4th Luftflotte.

Due to such an oversized assault device, the primary objectives of the offensive were achieved with relative ease. Although sustaining significant losses, Seydlitz's 51st Corps completed a decisive maneuver, once again splitting the Soviet forces, depriving them of the Tractor Factory and isolating Group Gorokhov north of the Mechetka River. After two days only and despite desperate resistance the Red Army lines were devastated, 62nd Army's global strength reduced by 25% and defense capacity in northern Stalingrad dwindled by half.

However, the dramatic advance of the Wehrmacht's assault groups in the wake of the first onslaught had already began to slow down on the third day, and obviously waned after a week of merciless combats.

As a result and despite important territorial gains the morale of German troops, which was already not at its best, decreased even more whereas that of Soviet troops steadily increased.

The new task force led by 79th Infantry Division performs a limited yet costly advance against the salient of 193rd Rifle Division north of the Red October Metal Factory [1].

Intense close combat continues in the western part of the Barricades Gun Factory.

Other sectors: In other sectors the situation remains unchanged.

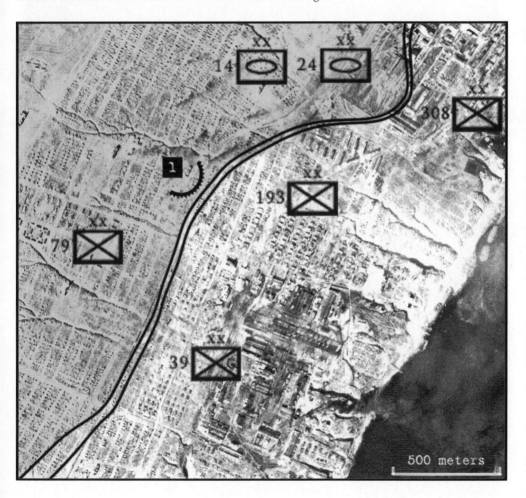

German MG-34 machinegun

The see-saw struggle in the western part of the Barricades Factory continues relentlessly. 138th Rifle Division is solidly entrenched in the whole complex **[1]** [1].

Other sectors: In the northern suburbs, Group Gorokhov still resists the incessant onslaught led by 14th Panzer Corps and involving 16th Panzer, 94th and part of 389th Division.

The Southwestern Front, which had been disbanded on July 12 in the wake of the Stalingrad Front creation, is now reformed under N.F. Vatutin and located west of the Don Front. Owing to efficient Soviet маскировка "maskirovka" - secrecy measures, German intelligence will fail to detect it for long.

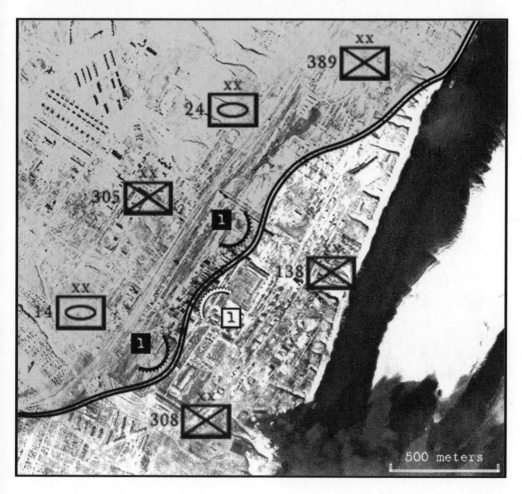

Soviet DP machinegun

The general offensive resumes with the Red October Factory as objective. On the northern flank, the group led by 14th Panzer Division progresses 100-200 meters only, pushing 685th Regiment back a few blocks and hardly reaching the Bread Factory, with severe losses for both sides.

Defending along the railroad, 895th Regiment denies access to the territory between the two factories.

The southern flank is far more successful: 79th Division breaks trough Soviet lines at the joint between 193rd and 39th Divisions. Its two regiments subsequently occupy a large part of the Red October Factory complex and about 2/3 of its halls and shops. 208th Regiment invests the factory's central part [1], 212th Regiment invests the southern section [2] whereas separate companies momentarily reach the Volga [3].

Other sectors: In other sectors the situation remains unchanged.

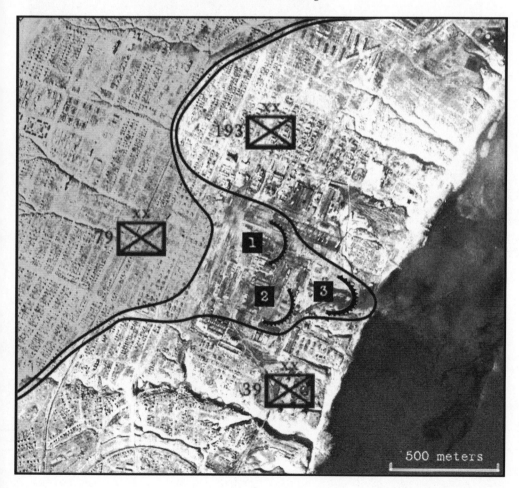

German infantry crawling in factory shops

★ *Major-General N.I. Krylov, 62ⁿᵈ Army Chief of Staff:*

Beginning October 23, the "Red October" factory became the enemy's main target. It was the oldest of the three Stalingrad industrial giants and the last yet untouched by Nazi soldiers. It was not difficult for us to imagine that the enemy, stuck in the "Barricades" factory, would try to break through on the neighboring sector. There appeared Schwerin's 79th Infantry Division, which previously operated against the Don front. It was known that this elite division had been recently reinforced [...] Defending the factory also meant protecting the Volga landing stage, without which the army could not exist. The main defending force was Major-General Guriev's 39th Guards Division. Major-General Smekhotvorov's 193rd Rifle Division, by this time reduced to a third of its normal strength, was also by the "Red October" with its left flank. The Germans began their offensive with a night attack, which was repelled. In the morning, after a powerful artillery preparation, infantry and tanks attacked several areas at once on the right wing of the army. It was soon determined that the main strike was aimed at the factory, towards which the enemy put forward its new division. It looked almost the same as a week before: the bombing was just as tremendous and caused the greater part of our casualties. Communications were broken, but due to our proximity we were able to maintain connection with Guriev and Smekhotvorov. And one could only say that they fought valiantly.[2]

✚ *Wehrmacht GHQ information report for 23.10.1942:*

In Stalingrad, 79th Infantry Division captured the railroad in the metallurgical plant's western part and its shock groups reached the central yards. Large factory workshops were captured. The fighting continues. According to unconfirmed reports, one assault group has broken through to the Volga. 14th Panzer Division also eliminated pockets of resistance in the Bread Factory. Bombers conducted massive strikes on enemy positions. In addition, our aircraft continued to raid enemy artillery positions on the Volga islands and east bank. Diversionary attacks in the northern part of the city were repelled.[3]

Ten days after the beginning of the October offensive German forces are utterly exhausted, particularly on the northern flank of the attacking device, where 305th Division, 24th and most of 14th Panzer Divisions are now bled white and have lost most of their tanks.

The still effective 79th Division tries to continue large-scale maneuvers within the Red October Factory, but succeeds only in grinding down some more terrain.

208th Regiment gains part of a great hall in the northern sector [1] whereas 212th Regiment gains some more workshops in the southern sector [2]. The incursion on the Volga bank is liquidated in a counterattack by 39th Guards Division's 117th Regiment [1].

Other sectors: In other sectors the situation remains unchanged.

Tangled metal structures in a hall invested by the Wehrmacht

★ *Soviet national newspaper "Pravda":*

The enemy is again concentrating his main forces in the industrial area. Almost without a break, heavy bombs are being dropped on the factories. The enemy is attacking with superior forces. We are forced to fight in difficult conditions. The enemy has not only superior strength, but holds more advantageous positions. His communications are invisible from the ground. We have to communicate with the rear under the Germans' very noses. Even so, we are standing firm. But it is difficult. In the last twenty-four hours, the Germans attacked the factories in even greater strength than before. They have brought up one more tank division and have been advancing with, altogether, four infantry and two tank divisions.[3]

✚ *German national newspaper "Deutsche Algemeine Zeitung":*

A cruel battle is fought for every inch of ground. Our soldiers, worn out, with hollow cheeks and eyes red for lack of sleep, are praying for an end of the battle. Stalingrad is a hell. The Bolsheviks are putting up desperately bitter resistance, with nothing equal to it.[3]

✚ *W. Hoffman, soldier in 94ᵗʰ Infantry Division:*

Who would have thought three months ago that instead of the joy of victory we would have to endure such sacrifice and torture, the end of which is nowhere in sight? The soldiers are calling Stalingrad the mass grave of the Wehrmacht. There are very few men left in the companies. We have been told we are soon going to be withdrawn to be brought back up to strength.[4]

In the Red October complex, 208th Regiment's forces try to push on through the northern part's buildings but face a violent counterattack from the remainder of 39th Guards Division's 112th Regiment. As a result, the positions stabilize on the previous day's boundaries.

While on both sides regimental effective strength rarely exceeds 50 men, the struggle for the Barricades, Red October and Bread Factories, with the land in between, continues day and night.

Other sectors: Eremenko directs Shumilov's 64th Army (30,000 men) to attack Stalingrad's suburbs from the south in order to draw there some of the German forces from the factories district. Though supported by a significant number of tanks, artillery and aircraft, the Soviets fail to pierce through 371st Division's lines.

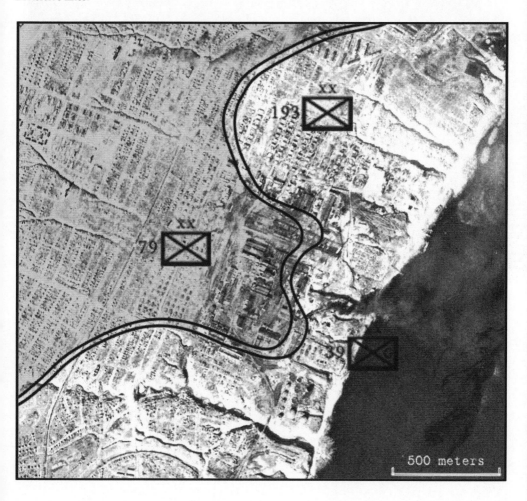

Soviet soldiers with PPSh-41 sub machineguns

6th Army's Command directs its depleted assault groups to carry on the offensive with what was left of their offensive strength, concentrating on the narrow sector between the last two factories standing, where Soviet forces are reduced to separate strongholds with no solid boundaries.

The last able elements of 14th Panzer Division succeed in overpowering the remaining part of the Bread Factory [1]. Continuing the action, in a bold move which takes the scattered elements of 193rd Rifle Division by surprise, an advanced group of about 50 panzer grenadiers assisted by some tanks pushes on right up to the Volga, threatening to disable the last Soviet landing stage [2].

Other sectors: In other sectors the situation remains unchanged.

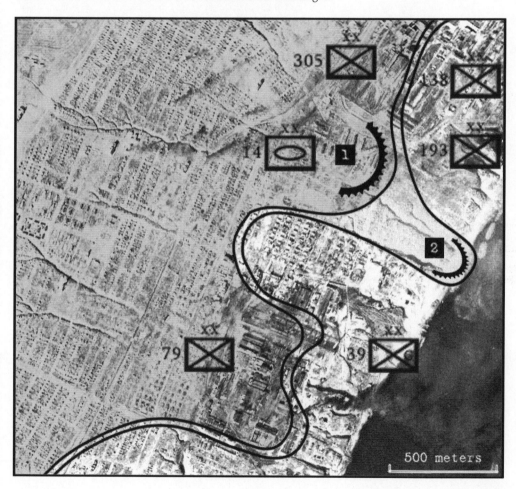

Germans section peering cautiously at their target

Schwerin's 79th Division receives back its 226th Regiment which rejoins the other two regiments already fighting in the city, so their advance inside the Red October Factory can continue [1].

Assessing the utmost danger of the situation that just created around the last valid landing stage, Chuikov forms a special detachment by scrapping up the last available men in the sector. Along with three patched-up tanks, they succeed in driving back the panzer grenadiers from the river bank [1].

Sokolov's 45th Rifle Division begins to cross the Volga as a last reinforcement to 62nd Army. Due to the proximity of the frontline and the hazardous use of what remains of the landing stage, its units arrive to the city by parcels only, performing long bypassing journeys for three days on

Other sectors: In other sectors the situation remains unchanged.

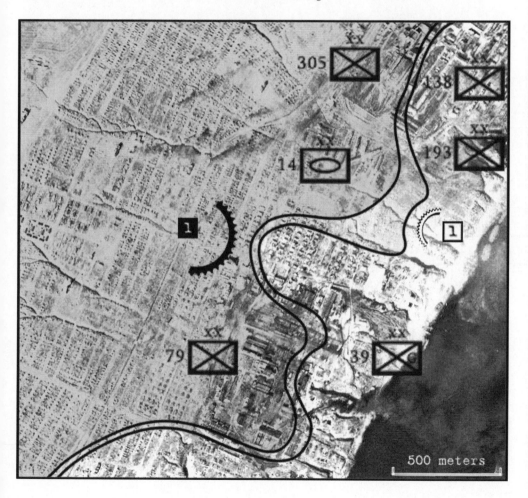

★ *Lieutenant-General V.I. Chuikov, 62ⁿᵈ Army Commander*

On October 27, the left flank of Liudnikov's division was crushed by the enemy, which began shelling our last crossing zone. Nazi machine-gunners reached 39th Division's HQ, hand grenades began to fly into Guriev's dugout. I immediately sent a company of our own HQ security to the rescue. Fending off the attack, it pursued the enemy right into the "Red October" plant [...] Ravines leading to the Volga were subjected to direct fire. Our engineers eventually raised wood and stones fences across the gullies. Then elements of Sokolov's 45th Division began arriving. During the night we managed to get across only two battalions [...] [1]

★ *V.P. Nekrassov, engineer battalion Deputy Commander:*

There were times when our reinforcements looked really pathetic. They'd bring across the river, with great difficulty, some twenty new soldiers: either old chaps of fifty or fifty-five, or youngsters of eighteen or nineteen. They would stand there on the shore, shivering with cold and fear. They'd be given warm clothing and then taken to the front line. By the time these newcomers reached this line, five or ten out of twenty had already been killed by German shells [...] But the peculiar thing about these chaps was that those who reached the frontline very quickly became wonderfully hardened soldiers, real "frontoviks".[4]

✚ *J. Shafshtein, NCO in 226th Regiment, 79th Infantry Division:*

It's a real inferno there! Today I saw the Volga for the first time. Our attacks are unsuccessful: the offensive, which at first yielded good hopes, is now regressing. There was such a heavy bombing at night that we thought this was the end... The following day our assault failed again, the enemy is firing from all around, from every slit and crevice. It's impossible to move. At night we're harassed by Russian aviation, artillery and "Katyushas". Losses are high.[4]

6ᵀᴴ ARMY

CHIEF OF STAFF
Arthur Schmidt

COMMANDER
Friedrich Paulus

CHIEF OF OPERATIONS
Wilhelm Adam

L 14ᵀᴴ PANZER CORPS

COMMANDER
Hans-Valentin Hube

60ᵀᴴ MOTORIZED DIVISION
Otto Kohlermann

3ᴿᴰ MOTORIZED DIVISION
Helmuth Schlömer

16ᵀᴴ PANZER DIVISION
Günther Angern

L 51ˢᵀ ARMY CORPS

COMMANDER
Walther von Seydlitz-Kurzbach

94ᵀᴴ INFANTRY DIVISION
Georg Pfeiffer

389ᵀᴴ INFANTRY DIVISION
Erwin Jänecke

24ᵀᴴ PANZER DIVISION
Arno von Lenski

305ᵀᴴ INFANTRY DIVISION
Kurt Oppenländer

14ᵀᴴ PANZER DIVISION
Ferdinand Heim

79ᵀᴴ INFANTRY DIVISION
Richard von Schwerin

100ᵀᴴ JAGER DIVISION
Werner Sanne

L 48ᵀᴴ PANZER CORPS

COMMANDER
Werner Kempf

295ᵀᴴ INFANTRY DIVISION
Rolf Wuthmann

71ˢᵀ INFANTRY DIVISION
Alexander von Hartmann

29ᵀᴴ MOTORIZED DIVISION
Hans-Georg Leyser

62ⁿᵈ ARMY

CHIEF OF STAFF
Nikolay Krylov

COMMANDER
Vasily Chuikov

POLITICAL OFFICER
Kuzma Gurov

GROUP GOROKHOV

124ᵀᴴ RIFLE BRIGADE
Sergey Gorokhov

149ᵀᴴ RIFLE BRIGADE
Vasily Bolvinov

ARMY UNITS

138ᵀᴴ RIFLE DIVISION
Ivan Liudnikov

308ᵀᴴ RIFLE DIVISION
Leonty Gurtiev

193ᴿᴰ RIFLE DIVISION
Fedor Smekhotvorov

45ᵀᴴ RIFLE DIVISION
Vasily Sokolov

235ᵀᴴ TANK BRIGADE
Denis Burdov

39ᵀᴴ GRD RIFLE DIVISION
Stepan Guriev

284ᵀᴴ RIFLE DIVISION
Nikolay Batiuk

13ᵀᴴ GRD RIFLE DIVIS
Aleksandr Rodimtse

Approximate unit strength of units attacking the city or vicinity, from north to south

60th Motorized Infantry Division (30 tanks)	9,000
3rd Motorized Infantry Division (30 tanks)	7,000
16th Panzer Division (50 tanks)	6,000
94th Infantry Division	8,000
14th Panzer Corps total	30,000
Part of which actually facing Stalingrad (20 tanks)	12,000
389th Infantry Division	4,000
24th Panzer Division (15 tanks)	3,000
305th Infantry Division	7,500
14th Panzer Division (10 tanks)	5,000
79th Infantry Division	8,000
100th Jäger Division	6,000
295th Infantry Division	7,000
51st Army Corps total (25 tanks, 10 assault guns)	40,500
71st Infantry Division	8,500
48th Panzer Corps total	8,500
Total German 6th Army forces (55 tanks and AG)	61,000

Approximate unit strength of units defending the city or vicinity, from north to south

124th Rifle Brigade	2,500
149th Rifle Brigade	2,000
Group Gorokhov total	4,500
138th Rifle Division	2,000
308th Rifle Division	1,000
193th Rifle Division	2,000
45th Rifle Division	6,500
39th Guards Rifle Division	3,000
284th Rifle Division	4,000
13th Guards Rifle Division	5,000
Other Army-related formations and services	2,000
Total Soviet 62nd Army forces (10 tanks)	30,000

RED OCTOBER

After the initial assault wave completely spent itself, when it became clear that German troops were checked in the Barricades Factory and that it would not fall as easily as the Tractor Plant did, the main offensive axis shifted slightly southwards, targeting the Red October Factory and the adjacent 62nd Army's landing stage. By this time both sides were reinforced with the last possible reserves.

On German side Schwerin's 79th Infantry Division joined 51st Army Corps in order to lead the new advance, but it was evident that no other formation could be taken any more from the Don frontline without severely endangering 6th Army's flanks.

On Soviet side Liudnikov's 138th Rifle Division arrived just in time to man defensive positions on 62nd Army's northern front in the city, which by now ran just above the Barricades Factory and through the complex itself, while Sokolov's 45th Rifle Division brought substantial strength regarding the battle's standards. However, it crossed the Volga with difficulty and was the last formation to join 62nd Army in Stalingrad.

Indeed November was approaching followed by its first snowfalls and ice flows, which appeared to the defenders as an even greater danger than the new German division, for it would completely severe their already fragile supply lines across the great river.

Nevertheless, despite ever more difficult conditions, Red Army Commanders and soldiers rejoiced by noticing a significant change in their opponent's behavior. They could now see that the enemy attacks consisted no longer in coordinated operations but were rather like single outbursts of action and attempts to move in undetermined directions. It was obvious that the German war machine had become increasingly deranged and that its components were in a general state of degradation.

Packed together in the two kilometer part of land between the factories, remnants of 685th, 883rd and 895th Regiments of Smekhotvorov's 193rd Division now backed up by 10th Regiment of Sokolov's 45th Rifle Division [1] desperately defend the badly damaged landing stage against assault groups from Heim's 14th Panzer Division [1].

The remaining assault forces of 576th, 577th and 578th Regiments of Oppenländer's 305th Division gain ground inside the Barricades Factory, driving back what was left of 344th, 650th and 768th Regiments of Liudnikov's 138th Division along with the few soldiers of 339th and 347th Regiments from Gurtiev's severely depleted 308th Division [2].

German pressure continues within the Red October Factory, two more halls are taken from 120th Regiment of Guriev's 39th Guards Division in the northern part of the complex [3].

Other sectors: In other sectors the situation remains unchanged.

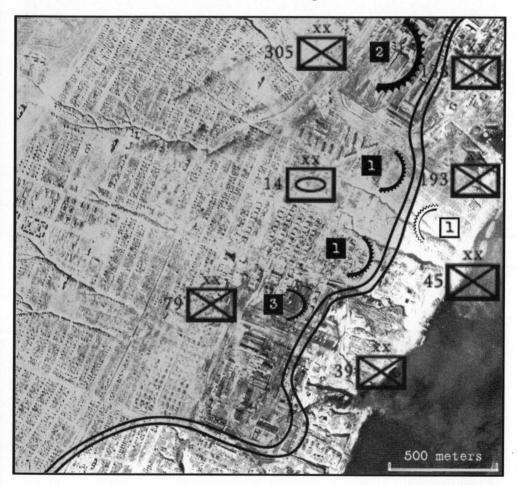

Soviet soldiers inside the ruined factory halls

★ *V.S. Grossman, war press correspondent:*

One cannot help wondering how such resilience was forged. Different aspects were telling there: a national sense, a feeling of great responsibility, a sullen, sturdy Siberian perseverance, an excellent military and political training with strict discipline. But I would like to add one more feature, which played a significant role in this great epic: the amazing, unaffected morality and strong comradeship that bound together the men of the Siberian division. A Spartan spirit of modesty characterizes the division's commanders. It is felt in everyday little things, in the refusal of the appointed 100 grams of vodka throughout the entire battle, in an inconspicuous but rational activity. I witnessed these people's solidarity in their sorrow when speaking about lost comrades. I saw it during a touching meeting between Colonel Gurtiev and nurse Zoia Kalganova, coming back to the battalion after her second wounding. "Hello my dear girl" said Gurtiev quietly, and with outstretched hands he quickly went toward the skinny girl with short hair, like a father meeting his daughter. This love and faith in each other enabled simple soldiers to assist and replace commanders when necessary, whereas staff officers did not hesitate to take up a machine gun, a hand grenade, a flammable liquid bottle to repel tanks attacks near the command posts.[5]

✠ *W. Hoffman, soldier in 94ᵗʰ Infantry Division:*

Our troops have captured the whole of the Barricades factory, but we cannot break through to the Volga. The Russians are not men, but some kind of cast-iron creatures, they never get tired and are not afraid of fire. We are absolutely exhausted, our regiment has now barely the strength of a company. The Russian artillery on the other side of the Volga won't let you lift your head. Each soldier sees himself as a condemned man. The only hope is to be wounded and taken back rear.[4]

Soviet forces in the Barricades Factory are finally overcome, their remnants now cling to the small strip of land running along the Volga behind [1].

14th Panzer Division's assault groups maintain a strong pressure, grinding down Soviet defenses in front of 62nd Army's last Volga crossing sector [2].

Other sectors: Despite an exceptionally concentrated bombing and repeated assaults, German forces are unable to break the last stronghold in the northern part of the Red October Factory.

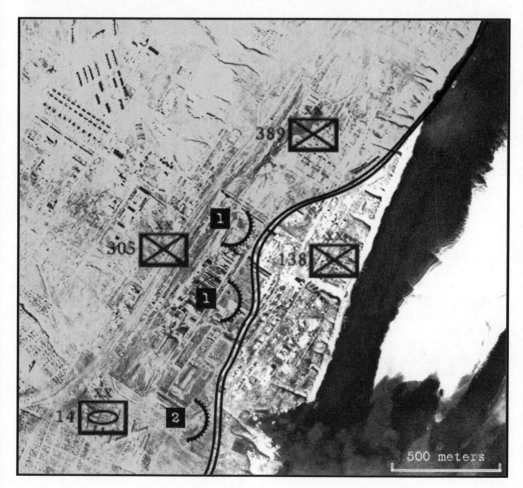

Panzer III kurz, industrial sector

The German offensive is once again utterly exhausted, whereas opposed 45th Rifle Division has now completed its crossing and its men are firmly entrenched in the sector of the landing stage. The Soviet command is confident that Stalingrad will hold at last. North of the factories, events had proved that group Gorokhov would also last, and could even lead counterattacks on its own, inflicting huge losses on the enemy.

Newly arrived troops of 45th Rifle Division's 253rd Regiment begin a joint operation with remnants from 39th Guards Division in order to regain terrain within the Red October Factory's northern section [1].

Other sectors: In other sectors the situation remains unchanged.

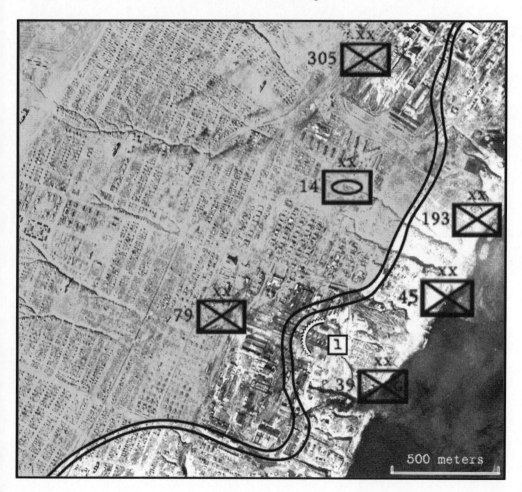

Red Army soldier with canteen and PPSh-41 sub machinegun

Soviet troops continue to push back the Germans, regaining some terrain and workshops within the Red October Factory [1].

Other sectors: A Soviet commando operation across the river in the Latashinka sector, north of the beleaguered Group Gorokhov, fails tragically under strong enemy fire.

Soviet assault group in the Red October Factory

★ *Soviet Army newspaper Red Star, 31.10.1942:*

During all of October, the Germans kept on attacking the northern part of the city, the factory district of Stalingrad. They dropped tens of thousands of bombs on the industrial area and the workers' settlements. Throughout the month, they methodically shelled the northern part of the city with artillery and mortars. It is difficult to count how many attacks were fought off in this sector. A single rifle division reflected 32 major German attacks supported by tanks and aircraft during 20 days in October. Hundreds of guardsmen displayed great valor in these fights [...] Suffering heavy losses and having failed to achieve significant progress, the enemy has reduced his activity. Whereas two days ago he was still trying to advance with one and a half infantry and one tank divisions in the factory area, yesterday and today the Germans committed a much smaller infantry and tank force. Their artillery fire also became somewhat weaker. To a certain extent, this was due to the increasing activity of our bomber and ground attack aircraft, which were striking day and night enemy mechanized units, artillery and supply routes.[3]

✠ *W. Hoffman, soldier in 94th Infantry Division:*

In the last few days our battalion has several times tried to attack the Russian positions to no avail. On this sector also the Russians won't let you lift your head. There have been a number of cases of self-inflicted wounds and malingering among the men. Every day I write two or three reports about them.[4]

83

Intense fighting continues in the sector between the Barricades and Red October factories where German units, although depleted, are still trying to reach the Volga banks.

A new German attempt to force the way toward the landing stage is warded off by Soviet defenders [1].

Other sectors: 64th Army's progression in the southern suburbs is definitely checked. After a seven-day offensive Soviet assault groups have advanced no more than 2 kilometers and failed to attract new German forces from the northern sector of the city.

★ *Major-General N.I. Krylov, 62ⁿᵈ Army Chief of Staff:*

November had come. The nights became much colder. In these steppe lands severe frosts arrive suddenly, and no one could accurately determine when the Volga will begin to freeze. Natives of these places just warned that no frost can deal immediately with the great river, that freezing usually delayed, and that some years the Volga cannot be crossed for a long time, either by boat or by foot. Of course, it was necessary to think in advance about the changes in the army's situation when the river will finally freeze. For example, which measures need to be taken in order to prevent any outflanking enemy maneuver on the ice, but first of all how to fulfill the needs in supplies during freeze-up time, when communications with the left bank, already difficult, may be severed and the army cut off from its supply bases for an indefinite period. To feel more confident, it was necessary to store more ammunition and try to create at least some kind of fighting reserve. What could be done and how: this question was more than once discussed by the Military council.[2]

✚ *Wehrmacht GHQ information report for 01.11.1942:*

South of Stalingrad the enemy again counterattacked unsuccessfully. An attempt by several Soviet battalions to cross the Volga north of Stalingrad completely failed. A large number of boats were sunk, most of the Russian forces were destroyed or captured. Our aircraft destroyed enemy artillery positions on the eastern bank of the Volga. North of Astrakhan, as a result of our bombing, 13 military trains were destroyed.[3]

After minor restructuration and reinforcement, 305th Division's assault groups try to resume their advance against Soviet troops defending beyond the Barricades Factory, but the attack comes rapidly to a stall, the Germans progress no more than 100 meters [1].

Refitted 161st and 241st Regiments of Gorishny's 95th Rifle Division cross the river and reinforce 62nd Army's defenses behind the factories [1].

Other sectors: In other sectors the situation remains unchanged.

Soviet defense position receiving ammunition

With both sides utterly exhausted, it becomes once again obvious that there would be no further offensive in the next days. A week-long lull installs on the whole front, each side reorganizing and consolidating its positions, occasionally conducting reconnaissance missions.

Other sectors: In other sectors the situation remains unchanged.

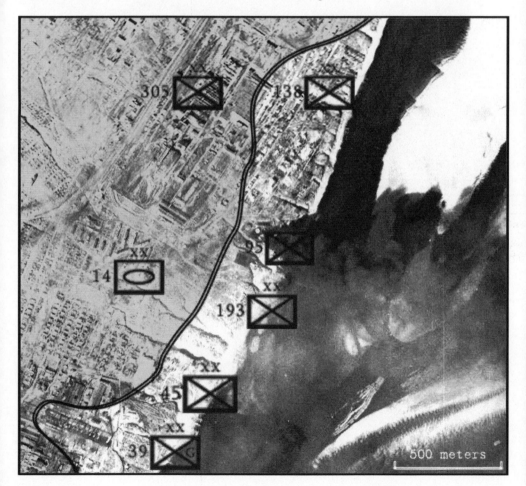

In the destroyed Red October plant complex

6ᵀᴴ ARMY

CHIEF OF STAFF
Arthur Schmidt

COMMANDER
Friedrich Paulus

CHIEF OF OPERATIONS
Wilhelm Adam

L 14ᵀᴴ PANZER CORPS

COMMANDER
Hans-Valentin Hube

60ᵀᴴ MOTORIZED DIVISION
Otto Kohlermann

3ᴿᴰ MOTORIZED DIVISION
Helmuth Schlömer

16ᵀᴴ PANZER DIVISION
Günther Angern

L 51ˢᵀ ARMY CORPS

COMMANDER
Walther von Seydlitz-Kurzbach

94ᵀᴴ INFANTRY DIVISION
Georg Pfeiffer

389ᵀᴴ INFANTRY DIVISION
Erich Magnus

24ᵀᴴ PANZER DIVISION
Arno von Lenski

305ᵀᴴ INFANTRY DIVISION
Bernhard Steinmetz

14ᵀᴴ PANZER DIVISION
Ferdinand Heim

79ᵀᴴ INFANTRY DIVISION
Richard von Schwerin

100ᵀᴴ JAGER DIVISION
Werner Sanne

L 48ᵀᴴ PANZER CORPS

COMMANDER
Werner Kempf

295ᵀᴴ INFANTRY DIVISION
Rolf Wuthmann

71ˢᵀ INFANTRY DIVISION
Alexander von Hartmann

29ᵀᴴ MOTORIZED DIVISION
Hans-Georg Leyser

62nd ARMY

CHIEF OF STAFF
Nikolay Krylov

COMMANDER
Vasily Chuikov

POLITICAL OFFICER
Kuzma Gurov

L GROUP GOROKHOV

124TH RIFLE BRIGADE
Sergey Gorokhov

149TH RIFLE BRIGADE
Vasily Bolvinov

L ARMY UNITS

138TH RIFLE DIVISION
Ivan Liudnikov

308TH RIFLE DIVISION
Leonty Gurtiev

193RD RIFLE DIVISION
Fedor Smekhotvorov

45TH RIFLE DIVISION
Vasily Sokolov

39TH GRD RIFLE DIVISION
Stepan Guriev

95TH RIFLE DIVISION
Vasily Gorishny

284TH RIFLE DIVISION
Nikolay Batiuk

13TH GRD RIFLE DIVISIO
Aleksandr Rodimtsev

Approximate unit strength of units attacking the city or vicinity, from north to south

60th Motorized Infantry Division (30 tanks)	8,000
3rd Motorized Infantry Division (30 tanks)	6,500
16th Panzer Division (50 tanks)	5,000
94th Infantry Division	7,000
14th Panzer Corps total	**26,500**
Part of which actually facing Stalingrad (20 tanks)	11,000
389th Infantry Division	6,000
24th Panzer Division (10 tanks)	4,000
305th Infantry Division	6,000
14th Panzer Division (10 tanks)	5,000
79th Infantry Division	7,500
100th Jäger Division	5,500
295th Infantry Division	7,500
51st Army Corps total (40 tanks, 10 assault guns)	41,500
71st Infantry Division	8,000
48th Panzer Corps total	8,000
Total German 6th Army forces (50 tanks and AG)	60,000

Approximate unit strength of units defending the city or vicinity, from north to south

124th Rifle Brigade	2,000
149th Rifle Brigade	1,000
Group Gorokhov total	3,000
138th Rifle Division	1,500
308th Rifle Division	500
193th Rifle Division	1,000
45th Rifle Division	5,000
39th Guards Rifle Division	2,500
284th Rifle Division	3,500
13th Guards Rifle Division	4,000
Other Army-related formations and services	2,000
Total Soviet 62nd Army forces	23,000

STABILIZATION

The battle for the factory district continues, although conditions are now completely different from what they were two weeks ago at the beginning of the offensive.

The attrition on both sides is so severe that often a division's frontline strength is actually reduced to that of a battalion, while regiments become equivalent to companies. Though still resembling to significant units on situation maps, the real state of the opposing forces in the city is appalling.

The troops still fit for fighting and actually manning the frontline in Stalingrad now amount to a bare 20,000 men on German side against 15,000 men on Soviet side. Attackers and defenders share the same miserable state. Both are completely exhausted and under-supplied. As usual since the beginning of the battle, the defenders had been reinforced at the most critical moments. Deprived of their objectives when it seemed they would fall into their hands, the Germans end fully demoralized in addition. Regarding the armor, scarcely more than thirty tanks and assault guns are still able to support 51st Corps's assaults groups inside the city, while on Soviet side there are virtually no more vehicles left at all.

Whereas 6th Army's offensive effort still persisted in the last days of October and on the first few days of November, it was absolutely clear that there would be no major change on the front until further arrangements for the fighting troops.

Chuikov and his staff feel that 62nd Army has passed the test of strength, and that the worst is definitely over. Though Soviets troops control hardly 10% of Stalingrad and new difficulties are still to be expected for supplies, there is an overall confidence that Stalingrad will not fall now if it has not fallen before.

Beginning on November 4, a general lull installs once again in the ruined city, both opponents replenishing, regrouping and reorganizing their meager forces.

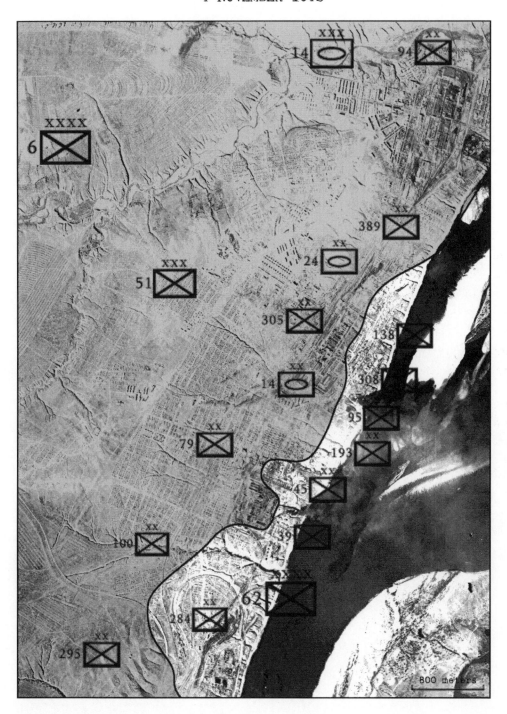

PREPARING FINAL ASSAULT

One week in November

04. 37th Guards Division's 118th Regiment, attached to 138th Rifle Division since the past 15 days, is now withdrawn across the Volga

Both sides limit their operations to reconnaissance and spoiling attacks between the Red October and Barricades factories

05. The Luftwaffe continues bombing actively what is left of Soviet positions in the industrial district as well as in the suburbs.

06. Mutual attacks by small assaults groups in the Red October Plant, fierce and costly, do not result in any significant gain

07. Duels of artillery from both sides of the Volga. Concentration of Soviet guns of every caliber on the eastern bank, with Front as well as Army units, is already more than a match for its German counterpart. Far more efficient than the Nebelwerfers, the Katyushas rocket launchers fire on enemy troops day and night.

08. Assessing this mighty potential, Army Group B orders bombing raids against Soviet artillery in Krasnaia Sloboda, which are scheduled to continue when permitted by the weather conditions.

09. Fighting only takes place in the Red October Factory.

Both sides continue regrouping and consolidating their positions

Hitler addresses senior members of the Nazi Party in as speech claiming possession of Stalingrad, mocking Soviet military power, and underscores that he will never leave the city.

German infantry supported by Panzer IV

The fighting resumes in the factory district. Foreboding a new offensive by Paulus, Chuikov directs a preventive strike in order to undermine his opponent's positions.

Guriev's 39th Guards Division attacks in the Red October Factory's southern sector where it recaptures a big hall and part of other shops [1].

Other sectors: In other sectors the situation remains unchanged.

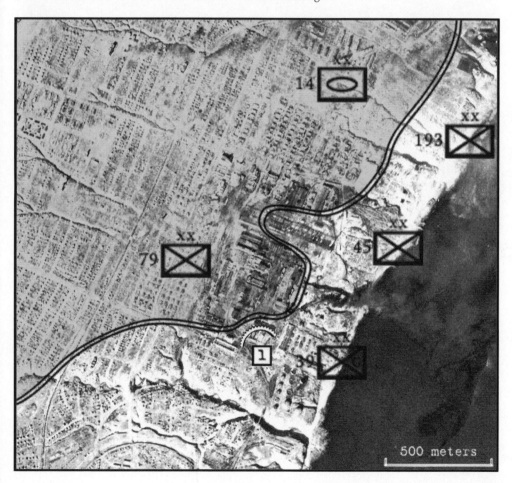

Red Army men at the top of a ruined structure

★ *V.S. Grossman, war press correspondent:*

Here, in Stalingrad, like nowhere else, one can see people who commit into war not only all their blood and flesh, but also all the power of their mind, all the stress of their thoughts. How many such men I met there - Colonels and Sergeants and Privates, thinking restlessly day and night about all the same, calculating something, sketching, as if these people defending the city had taken upon themselves the responsibility to develop an invention, to conduct research in the basements of a city where many brilliant professors and engineers' minds were recently doing the same in spacious academical and industrial laboratories [...] Just like the directors of Stalingrad's giant factories and the secretaries of district committees were proud that here, and in no other place, was working a famous Stakhanovite, Division commanders were now proud of their noble people.[5]

✠ *W. Hoffman, soldier in 94th Infantry Division:*

November 10. A letter from Elsa today. Everyone expects us home for Christmas. In Germany everyone believes we already hold Stalingrad. How wrong they are. If they could only see what Stalingrad has done to our army.[4]

✠ *Wehrmacht GHQ information report for 10.11.1942:*

In the eastern part of the metallurgical plant, the enemy supported by some tanks attacked again. The attacks were unsuccessful. Despite stubborn defense against our attacking troops, the enemy left the fuel depot as well as the northeastern portion of the gun factory.[3]

6ᵀᴴ ARMY

CHIEF OF STAFF
Arthur Schmidt

COMMANDER
Friedrich Paulus

CHIEF OF OPERATIONS
Wilhelm Adam

L 14ᵀᴴ PANZER CORPS

COMMANDER
Hans-Valentin Hube

60ᵀᴴ MOTORIZED DIVISION
Otto Kohlermann

3ᴿᴰ MOTORIZED DIVISION
Helmuth Schlömer

16ᵀᴴ PANZER DIVISION
Günther Angern

L 51ˢᵀ ARMY CORPS

COMMANDER
Walther von Seydlitz-Kurzbach

94ᵀᴴ INFANTRY DIVISION
Georg Pfeiffer

389ᵀᴴ INFANTRY DIVISION
Erich Magnus

24ᵀᴴ PANZER DIVISION
Arno von Lenski

305ᵀᴴ INFANTRY DIVISION
Bernhard Steinmetz

14ᵀᴴ PANZER DIVISION
Ferdinand Heim

79ᵀᴴ INFANTRY DIVISION
Richard von Schwerin

100ᵀᴴ JAGER DIVISION
Werner Sanne

L 48ᵀᴴ PANZER CORPS

COMMANDER
Werner Kempf

295ᵀᴴ INFANTRY DIVISION
Rolf Wuthmann

71ˢᵀ INFANTRY DIVISION
Alexander von Hartmann

29ᵀᴴ MOTORIZED DIVISION
Hans-Georg Leyser

62nd ARMY

CHIEF OF STAFF
Nikolay Krylov

COMMANDER
Vasily Chuikov

POLITICAL OFFICER
Kuzma Gurov

L GROUP GOROKHOV

124TH RIFLE BRIGADE
Sergey Gorokhov

149TH RIFLE BRIGADE
Vasily Bolvinov

L ARMY UNITS

138TH RIFLE DIVISION
Ivan Liudnikov

308TH RIFLE DIVISION
Leonty Gurtiev

95TH RIFLE DIVISION
Vasily Gorishny

193RD RIFLE DIVISION
Fedor Smekhotvorov

45TH RIFLE DIVISION
Vasily Sokolov

39TH GRD RIFLE DIVISION
Stepan Guriev

284TH RIFLE DIVISION
Nikolay Batiuk

13TH GRD RIFLE DIVISIO
Aleksandr Rodimtsev

Approximate unit strength of units attacking the city or vicinity, from north to south

60th Motorized Infantry Division (30 tanks)	7,000
3rd Motorized Infantry Division (30 tanks)	6,000
16th Panzer Division (50 tanks)	4,500
94th Infantry Division	6,000
14th Panzer Corps total	23,500
Part of which actually facing Stalingrad (20 tanks)	9,500
389th Infantry Division	8,000
24th Panzer Division (10 tanks)	5,500
305th Infantry Division	4,500
14th Panzer Division (10 tanks)	5,000
79th Infantry Division	7,500
100th Jäger Division	5,500
295th Infantry Division	8,000
51st Army Corps total (40 tanks, 30 assault guns)	44,000
71st Infantry Division	7,000
48th Panzer Corps total	7,000
Total German 6th Army forces (70 tanks and AG)	60,500

Approximate unit strength of units defending the city or vicinity, from north to south

124th Rifle Brigade	1,500
149th Rifle Brigade	1,000
Group Gorokhov total	**2,500**
138th Rifle Division	1,500
308th Rifle Division	500
95th Rifle Division	2,000
92nd Rifle Brigade	3,000
193rd Rifle Division	1,000
45th Rifle Division	4,500
39th Guards Rifle Division	2,500
284th Rifle Division	3,500
13th Guards Rifle Division	4,000
Other Army-related formations and services	2,000
Total Soviet 62nd Army forces	**27,000**

THE LAST ASSAULT

During the past seven days there had been occasional exchanges of fire only, an incredibly quiet situation compared to Stalingrad's intensity standards. Now that Chuikov's 62nd Army is holding barely more land in the industrial district than in the southern sectors, where positions have remained roughly the same as a month ago, there is no place in the city where the distance between the Volga and the frontline exceeds a thousand meters.

After much arguing about the aims and directions for the next and probably last offensive within the city, and especially about where to find the badly needed troops for leading it, the German Command finally chose to reinforce Seydlitz's 51st Corps with seven engineer battalions, taken mainly out of other Army Group A and B formations, and to allocate twenty assault guns for close support. The engineers were not assembled together but dispatched between the different infantry companies.

Similarly to the lull preceding the last major assault and stressing the growing anxiety, there was a regain of activity towards the end of the period with both sides probing each other, preparing the terrain to begin the upcoming offensive in the best possible conditions.

Because of the ever reducing scale of operations, such objectives as single buildings were by now showing out not only at regimental or divisional levels on tactical maps, but even at corps and army levels on strategic maps, for Germans and Soviets sides alike. Moreover, any positive results regarding these limited targets were genuinely acclaimed as great achievements by soldiers on the ground as well as by HQ staff members.

While the battleground appeared more than ever like a nightmarish sight, with opposing troops squeezing each other amid an indescribable entanglement of stone rubble and iron wreckage, the fight for the last strip of land was about to begin.

6th Army's Command launches what it deems its final offensive in Stalingrad. Seydlitz's assault groups succeed in advancing significantly at the cost of numerous casualties and losing about half their tank force the first day.

Magnus's 389th Division, reinforced with three engineer battalions and assault guns, advances north of the Barricades Factory right up to the Volga, crushing Liudnikov's 138th Division's right wing [1].

Steinmetz's 305th Division, reinforced with four engineer battalions and supported by assault guns, advances from the factory's main body and reaches the fuel dumps near the river bank after wrecking 95th Division's 241st Regiment [2].

Other sectors: In other sectors the situation remains unchanged.

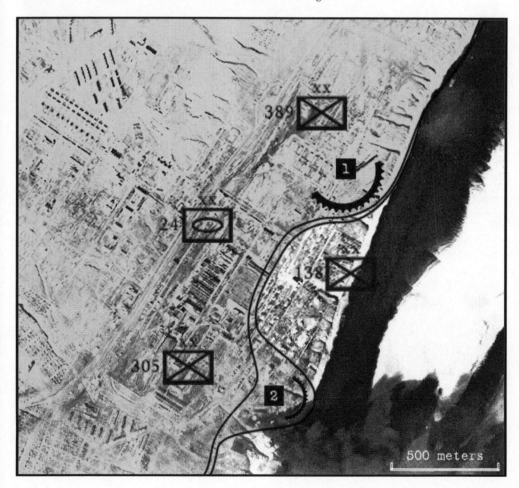

★ *Major-General N.I. Krylov, 62ⁿᵈ Army Chief of Staff:*

The increasing ice flow virtually denied us any communication with the Volga's left bank. Paulus was probably waiting for this moment to begin a new offensive [...] The first attack did not bring any decisive success and remained inconclusive [...] Only after committing his reserves was the enemy able to perform a major strike south of the "Barricades" factory [...] splitting our Army a third time. The isolated "island" that formed between the main forces of the army and the Northern Group ran 700 meters along the bank with a depth of 450 meters only. It included the northeastern part of the "Barricades", several adjacent streets and the slope leading down to the Volga, rugged with ravines. There was Liudnikov's 138th Division.[2]

★ *Colonel I.I. Liudnikov, 138th Division Commander:*

At 6:00 November 11, after 30 minutes of artillery shelling, the enemy began its offensive along the whole division's front with up to three regiments supported by engineer battalions. 544th and 546th Regiments were advancing on our division's right flank and center, while 577th Regiment was advancing on our division's left flank. During four hours of fierce fighting our units repelled all attacks and inflicted heavy losses on the Germans. Then our opponent committed fresh forces with 50th Engineer Battalion, which eventually broke through the scarce remnants of 118th Guards Regiment and reached the Volga. On the center, 344th Regiment was holding on against all assaults since the morning and late into the night. However by day's end the enemy had outflanked 768th Regiment and, after pushing back our neighboring [95th] division, reached the river in the sector of the already depleted 650th Regiment. We were cut from 62ⁿᵈ Army's main forces. At this moment our division had consumed almost all its ammunition and we resorted to captured enemy weapons: after our crushing of German 336th Engineer Battalion, we were provided with a great quantity of Braunings which now equipped most of our men.[5]

Part of 90th Rifle Regiment and 92nd Rifle Brigade cross the Volga back to the city after having been replenished on the other side.

While German forces regroup for the next jump, Chuikov launches a counterattack in the direction of Liudnikov's threatened sector, but fails to restore the positions lost the day before [1].

Other sectors: 79th Infantry Division regains the terrain lost the previous days in the southeastern part of the Red October Factory, but is unable to progress in its northern halls like planned. Part of 284th Rifle Division's forces is allocated to strengthen the front on the southern side of the Red October Factory. 193rd Rifle Division is virtually destroyed, its last 300 men are merged with 95th Rifle Division.

German position with MG-34 machinegun

The Germans concentrate on reducing the forces of Liudnikov's 138th Rifle Division, encircled by 305th and 389th Infantry Divisions behind the Barricades Factory.

544th and 546th Infantry Regiments gain some ground on 768th Rifle Regiment in the northern sector of the beleaguered "island" [1].

578th Infantry Regiment succeeds in perforating the defense in the sector of 344th and 650th Rifle Regiments and in taking the fortified Commissar house, near 138th Rifle Division's HQ. A counterattack led by Liudnikov and his staff stabilizes the situation [2].

Other sectors: In other sectors the situation remains unchanged.

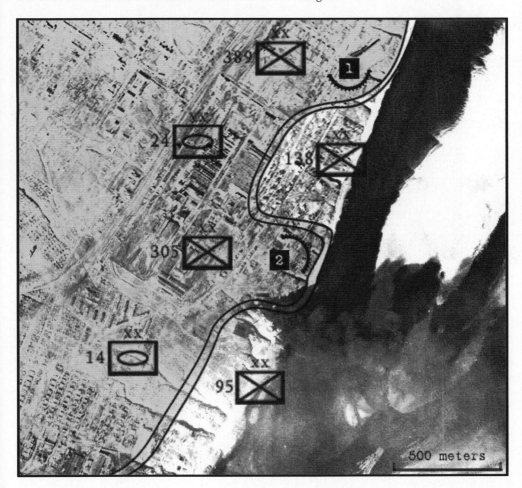

German infantry advancing

The battle has now cooled down along the entire front except at Liudnikov's island, whose 1,000 men are still assaulted by the 3,000 men of Steinmetz's 305th Infantry Division. Although outnumbered and running out of supplies, 138th Rifle Division occupies strong defensive positions with a fire radius over large patches of open terrain, and benefits from the full support of the artillery on the Volga's far side.

Supported by the whole of 51st Corps's remaining assault guns, 577th Infantry Regiment advances about 100 meters but the conquered terrain is for the most part taken back by units of 344th Rifle Regiment **[1]**.

Attacking in the sector of the oil tanks, Soviet forces try in vain to relieve the encircled troops [1].

Other sectors: In other sectors the situation remains unchanged.

Soviet Maxim light machinegun defense position inside Liudnikov's island

★ *Soviet Army newspaper Red Star:*

German offensive against the industrial area resumed some days ago. But this one was different from all previous offensives. If before, the Nazis attacked at several points simultaneously, now they attacked on a 200 to 400 meter wide front only. If before, they came up against a serious obstacle, they attacked elsewhere. Now they had decided to strike at one point all the time, a point which was, to them, the shortest cut to the Volga. Sappers were being used as infantry at the vanguard of German troops. The idea was to give the others greater confidence: sappers know more about mines and traps, and now they were advancing, carrying grenades and machine-guns. Then ordinary German infantry and tanks followed. In others parts of Stalingrad conditions are fairly quiet, but here the battle is furious... The enemy is taking advantage of the present state of the river which, with its ice floes, is rendering our supplies difficult. However, these difficulties are being overcome. The Germans have suffered heavy losses but their gains can be measured in meters...[5]

★ *Colonel I.I. Liudnikov, 138th Division Commander:*

We defended the "Barricades" sector for a hundred days and nights. And since November 11 until almost the end of the year, we were isolated from other army units. Before us and on our flanks was the enemy. Behind us was the river. In order to reach us from the other side of the Volga, one had to navigate under crossing fire from German machine guns. On these days, there was no mention of us in the papers because not one correspondent could come to us.[3]

German pressure on 138th Rifle Division continues but Soviet troops hold on and often counterattack.

578th Infantry Regiment succeeds in seizing a few more structures around the Commissar house [1].

546th Infantry Regiment continues compressing the positions of 768th Rifle Regiment [2].

Other sectors: In other sectors the situation remains unchanged.

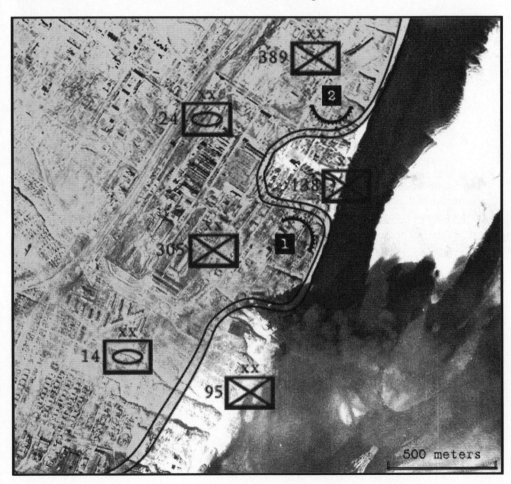

German mortar crew changing position

✚ *Fremde Heere Ost (Foreign Armies East) intelligence service:*

The enemy's intention to undertake an offensive in the sector of the allied armies, which had been already expected [by Army Group B], gradually emerges as more and more clear. Along with the detected assembly of two shock groups on the flanks of 3rd Romanian Army, where it must be assumed the enemy is ready to attack, there are growing signs of concentration of forces toward the west: radio communications with 63rd Army along with six or seven unknown divisions, presumed deployment of 1st Guard Army, heavy rail traffic and transfer of elements from 5th Tank Army. The overall picture of the group of forces in terms of location, time and quantity is not yet clear. There is no definitive evidence for a possible offensive yet. The assessment of the enemy's general intentions is impossible while this picture remains unclear. However, before long, an offensive should be expected against 3rd Romanian Army in order to block the road to Stalingrad, threaten the German troops located east, obtain the withdrawal of German troops around Stalingrad and restore traffic by water on the Volga. The forces currently available for the enemy are too weak for larger operations (there are about 16 infantry divisions and one to four armored brigades facing the right flank of 3rd Romanian Army, while seven infantry divisions and three cavalry divisions are facing the left flank). Nor is it yet clear whether to expect a major offensive across the Don against 8th Italian Army and 2nd Hungarian Army, which would then continue in the direction of Rostov, a move which could follow the operation against 3rd Romanian Army, or if the enemy would undertake offensive operations limited to the sectors of these three allied formations. The testimony of a captured officer, naming the Morozovsk-Stalingrad road as the goal of the offensive, seems to confirm this idea.[3]

Liudnikov's forces are now reduced to less than 500 men, half of them wounded and unfit for fighting. They can no longer be supplied through the Volga, but only by low-flying airplanes which occasionally manage to drop some supplies, part of which fall behind enemy lines due to the small size of the territory still controlled by 138th Rifle Division (400 by 300 meters). First snow is falling on Stalingrad.

Feeling uneasy about 6th Army's flank on the Don, the German High Command forms a mobile reserve with 22nd Panzer Division and Romanian 1st Armored Division, assigned to 48th Panzer Corps. Consisting mainly of outdated armor, this weak task force is in no way capable of dealing with large-scale operations.

Other sectors: In other sectors the situation remains unchanged.

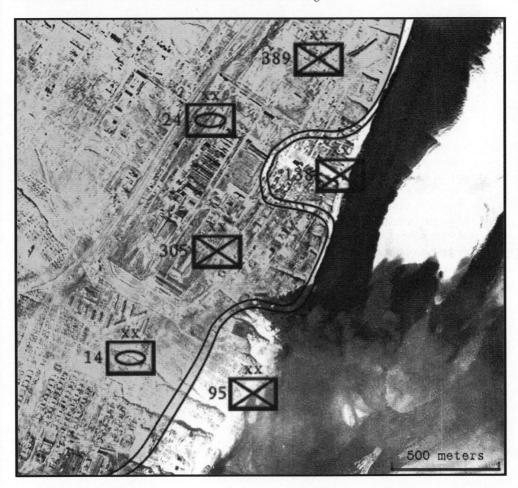

Soviet riflemen in defense position

62nd Army's main forces south of the Barricades Factory continue trying restlessly to break through to Liudnikov's besieged regiments.

After a strong artillery preparation, 95th Division moves forward and seizes the sector of the fuel tanks but cannot progress enough to link with 138th Division [1].

Other sectors: In other sectors the situation remains unchanged.

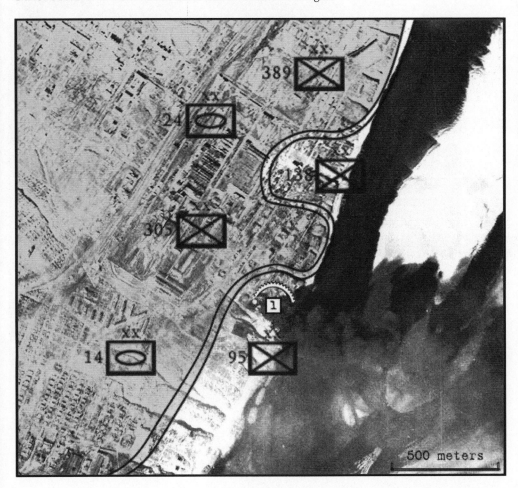

Soviet PPSh-41 submachine gunners defending a position

6TH ARMY

CHIEF OF STAFF
Arthur Schmidt

COMMANDER
Friedrich Paulus

CHIEF OF OPERATIONS
Wilhelm Adam

14TH PANZER CORPS

COMMANDER
Hans-Valentin Hube

60TH MOTORIZED DIVISION
Otto Kohlermann

3RD MOTORIZED DIVISION
Helmuth Schlömer

16TH PANZER DIVISION
Günther Angern

51ST ARMY CORPS

COMMANDER
Walther von Seydlitz-Kurzbach

94TH INFANTRY DIVISION
Georg Pfeiffer

389TH INFANTRY DIVISION
Erich Magnus

24TH PANZER DIVISION
Arno von Lenski

305TH INFANTRY DIVISION
Bernhard Steinmetz

14TH PANZER DIVISION
Ferdinand Heim

79TH INFANTRY DIVISION
Richard von Schwerin

100TH JAGER DIVISION
Werner Sanne

48TH PANZER CORPS

COMMANDER
Werner Kempf

295TH INFANTRY DIVISION
Otto Korfes

71ST INFANTRY DIVISION
Alexander von Hartmann

29TH MOTORIZED DIVISION
Hans-Georg Leyser

62nd ARMY

CHIEF OF STAFF
Nikolay Krylov

COMMANDER
Vasily Chuikov

POLITICAL OFFICER
Kuzma Gurov

GROUP GOROKHOV

124TH RIFLE BRIGADE
Sergey Gorokhov

149TH RIFLE BRIGADE
Vasily Bolvinov

ARMY UNITS

138TH RIFLE DIVISION
Ivan Liudnikov

308TH RIFLE DIVISION
Leonty Gurtiev

95TH RIFLE DIVISION
Vasily Gorishny

193RD RIFLE DIVISION
Fedor Smekhotvorov

45TH RIFLE DIVISION
Vasily Sokolov

39TH GRD RIFLE DIVISION
Stepan Guriev

284TH RIFLE DIVISION
Nikolay Batiuk

13TH GRD RIFLE DIVISIC
Aleksandr Rodimtsev

Approximate unit strength of units attacking the city or vicinity, from north to south

60th Motorized Infantry Division (30 tanks)	7,000
3rd Motorized Infantry Division (30 tanks)	7,000
16th Panzer Division (30 tanks)	5,500
94th Infantry Division	6,000
14th Panzer Corps total	25,500
Part of which actually facing Stalingrad (20 tanks)	10,000
389th Infantry Division	7,500
24th Panzer Division (50 tanks)	3,000
305th Infantry Division	4,500
14th Panzer Division (40 tanks)	6,500
79th Infantry Division	6,500
100th Jäger Division	6,000
295th Infantry Division	8,000
51st Army Corps total (110 tanks, 20 assault guns)	42,000
71st Infantry Division	7,000
48th Panzer Corps total	7,000
Total German 6th Army forces (130 tanks and AG)	59,000

Approximate unit strength of units defending the city or vicinity, from north to south

124th Rifle Brigade	1,000
149th Rifle Brigade	500
Group Gorokhov total	1,500
138th Rifle Division	500
308th Rifle Division	500
95th Rifle Division	1,000
193th Rifle Division	500
92nd Rifle Brigade	1,500
45th Rifle Division	3,500
39th Guards Rifle Division	2,000
284th Rifle Division	3,000
13th Guards Rifle Division	3,500
Other Army-related formations and services	2,000
Total Soviet 62nd Army forces	19,500

ON THE EVE OF A RED DAWN

If by mid-October the Wehrmacht's offensive operations have ceased along the entire Soviet front except in Stalingrad, by mid-November all troop activities inside the city settled down in turn, except around the small portion of land still held by 138th Rifle Division.

The press, which by now covers the events extensively, stresses the heroic resistance of these men cut off from the army and fighting their back on the Volga, so that all over Russia people speak about "Liudnikov's island". Short of everything, its remaining soldiers largely employ captured enemy weapons.

Given that the last possible reinforcements had already been dispatched to 62nd Army, Chuikov can only count on his own resources. The floating ice now severely restricts any traffic over the Volga and it becomes clear that soon no supplies at all could cross the river for the beleaguered defenders of Stalingrad.

But Paulus's troops are in no better shape. During this last stage of operations in the city, they had been compelled to organize themselves into no more than company-sized assault groups. The once almighty 6th Army has by now become a shadow of its original strength, fielding phantom units upon a frightful landscape.

While alarming reports continue to arrive from the Don front where the Red Army is gathering strong forces, the German Command still decides to regroup its assault troops once again, planning to resume the general offensive in the industrial district on November 20.

In the meantime 305th Infantry Division is directed to press on its attack against the last defenders behind the Barricades Factory.

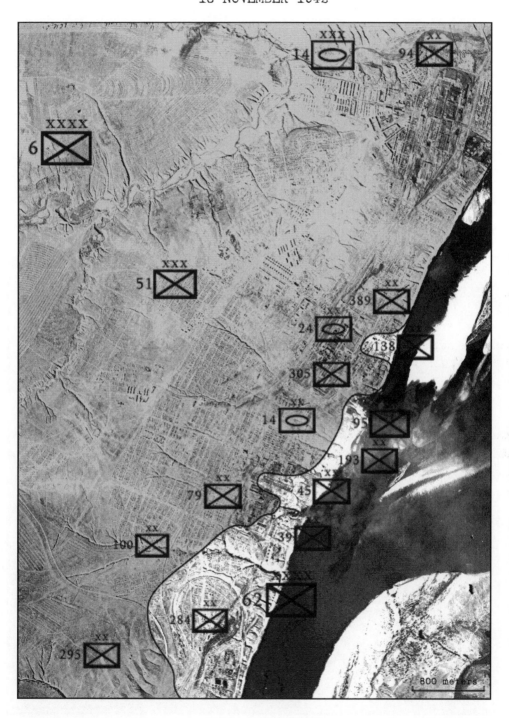

Whereas the situation becomes dramatic for Liudnikov's division, now completely deprived of supplies and with a growing number of wounded, German forces mount another local attack.

305th Division's 578th Regiment, supported by two engineer battalions and some tanks, progresses 200 meters further into 138th Division's positions [1].

This represents the last German advance within the city before the great Soviet counteroffensive.

Other sectors: In other sectors the situation remains unchanged.

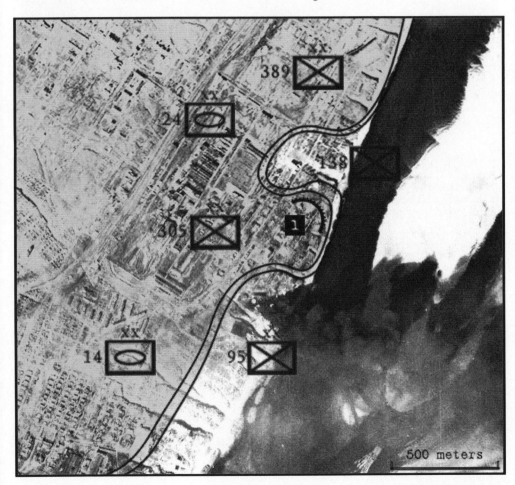

German troops receiving advancing orders

★ Lieutenant-General V.I. Chuikov, 62ⁿᵈ Army Commander

Late on November 18 we received the Front's directive: on the morning of November 19, the troops of the Southwestern and Don Fronts are beginning an offensive from the area of Kletskaya in the general direction of Kalach, the troops of the Stalingrad Front a day later, November 20, from the lakes area, Raygorod and Barmantsak in the general direction of Sovietsky then Kalach. Objective: to break the front of the enemy, to surround and destroy it. None of us was able to catch immediately the actual meaning of the impending events. It was an order to counterattack, to surround all the enemy forces concentrated around Stalingrad and to destroy them [...] It meant that the Supreme Command had been able to accumulate, assemble and deploy enormous forces. Our struggle for the city, our fierce resistance against the enemy in Stalingrad now acquired its ultimate sense. While the enemy bogged deeper and deeper into street battles, a formidable force grew on its flanks. Not vain was the bloodshed of Soviet soldiers, not vain was the defense of Stalingrad with our last strengths, when it seemed the Germans would crush us down. The slogans "Not a step back" and "No land for us beyond the Volga" took on new meaning. They now meant "Forward" and "Go west"! [1]

✚ General Der Panzertruppe F. Paulus, 6ᵗʰ Army Commander:

Under constant pressing from the OKW, our attacks were continuing. The attrition was such that six divisions fighting in Stalingrad were down to regiment strength level. In mid-September they occupied the southern part of the city, in October the northern part, reaching the Volga bank. The middle section was still in Russian hands. The separate fights from house to house which persisted until mid-November were no longer producing any substantial results because of the determined Russian resistance and incessant counterattacks. Since the end of August until the end of October, there was a constant pressure on the Army's northern front between Don and Volga, which fixed there the forces of XIV Panzer and VIII Army Corps, and included part of them in the fighting. [4]

Soviet nurses in the ruined city

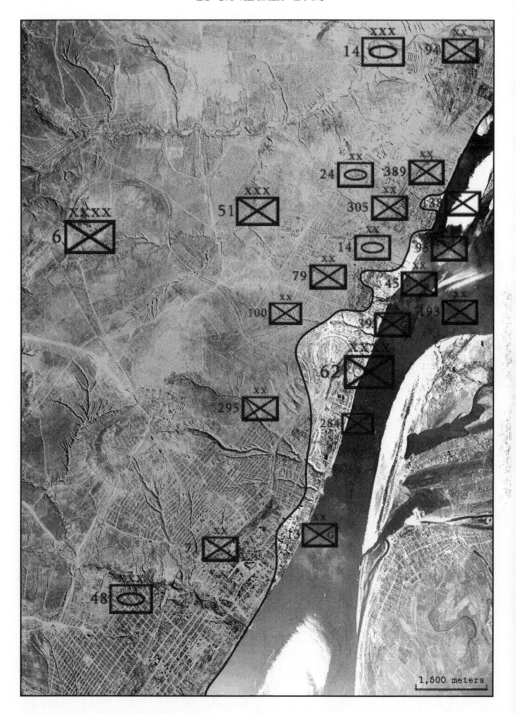

EPILOGUE

During seventy days fighting for Stalingrad, twelve German divisions have been completely bled white by their assault in the jagged ruins of the city, while ten others have eroded their strength dramatically in defensive battles between Don and Volga on 6th Army's northern flank, as well as on 4th Panzer Army's positions along the salt lakes, on the threshold of the Kalmyk Steppe.

Since no strategic value could be drawn any more out of the ruined city with Germans already controlling the greater part of it, there was no sense in continuing the assaults from a military perspective. All regular traffic on the Volga had been severed since September, and the Soviet oil route by river from the Caspian Sea to the rest of the country was no longer practicable. German forces were effectively locking up the near vicinity of Stalingrad, fending off all Soviet attacks directed towards Stalingrad and preventing any link with the city.

However, the distant flanks in the rear of the attacking armies were defended by poorly equipped units, consisting mainly of allied troops: Hungarian, Italian and Romanian, which followed the German advance and settled in these positions since late summer. Therefore, not even one of the two major objectives as initially devised for Plan Blau was achieved: the Wehrmacht troops in the Caucasus were still far from Baku and its petroleum, Army Group A and B supply lines were not secured yet. The logic would have commanded to extract the units still able from their grueling task in the city and use them to consolidate defense positions along the Don line in the north and around the salt lakes in the south.

But Hitler's obsession took over any military logic. It was far less a matter of strategy than of politics and demagogy. Promises had been solemnly made to the German people and repeated again and again by the press. For the past two months, the attention of the entire world had been focused on the city.

On Soviet side however, if it was also a matter of prestige, it was even more a question of strategy. While entire German divisions stubbornly persisted in their assault against the meager troops still defending Stalingrad, day after day and night after night, the Soviet High Command was building up formidable forces. If Chuikov received reinforcements with difficulty and even if the tactical forces ratio in and around the city was in favor of his opponent, the strategic picture in the whole region was quite different. The Red Army's reserves were steadily growing up while the forces available to Paulus were following an exactly inverse curve, slowly but surely melting away in the street fighting inferno.

If the central districts of the city had been taken after two weeks of heavy fighting, the other half including the industrial zone had required almost twice that time of raging assaults against an ever more desperate defense. Casualties for both sides were rising to dramatic levels. During the last thirty days, most of the combats had taken place in and around the Barricades and Red October factories, with opposing factions down to undersized battle groups of exhausted men, contesting such objects as a single basement or a machine-tool in a factory shop.

At the end of the entire defensive period, the Soviet-controlled territory was reduced to small pockets of resistance representing only one tenth of the urban area.

Stalingrad served as a giant trap for Hitler's obstinacy. Though it had been a meat grinder for the two opponents alike, the Wehrmacht could by no means win such a war of attrition. Germany's manpower and production capacity were already reaching their limits while Soviet resources were only beginning their reconstitution. The industries evacuated to the Urals were by now running at full speed, allowing new armies to be raised and provided with modern, adequate equipment and weapons, along with a great quantity of supplies and ammunition.

The assessment of the general strategic situation by the OKH intelligence services, by Paulus at army level, by Weichs at army group level, by Zeitzler at HQ level and first of all by Hitler himself, although acknowledging that several armies were indeed preparing an offensive and even perceiving its probable outbreak at the right time and place, yet completely underestimated the real Soviet potential, in terms of resources as well as leadership, for large-scale effective operations. Indeed since the beginning of the summer campaign, the Red Army had not been able to successfully perform any such kind of operation. Furthermore, the repeated setbacks of the Don Front against 6th Army's flanks during the whole period also largely contributed in misleading the German High Command on their adversary's actual capabilities.
However, this offensive had nothing in common with frontal attacks on limited objectives, led by unprepared and underequipped troops, a situation to which both sides were long accustomed to.

On November 19, the Don and Southwestern Fronts unleashed their forces from the bridgeheads on the Don northwest of the city. The day after, the Stalingrad Front did the same from the southeast. More than a million Soviet troops and a thousand tanks were rushing on, crushing everything in their advance. The long-awaited revenge had finally come. Operation Uranus had begun, which will end with the encirclement of the whole German 6th and Romanian 3rd Armies, part of 4th Panzer and 4th Romanian Armies, almost 350,000 men and an enormous quantity of materiel. It will lay the foundations for the entire Army Group B's destruction, and ultimately for the Red Army's victory over the Wehrmacht. From now on, the direction of the war will be only west.

ANNEXES

Extracts from wartime documents

GERMAN

DOCUMENTS

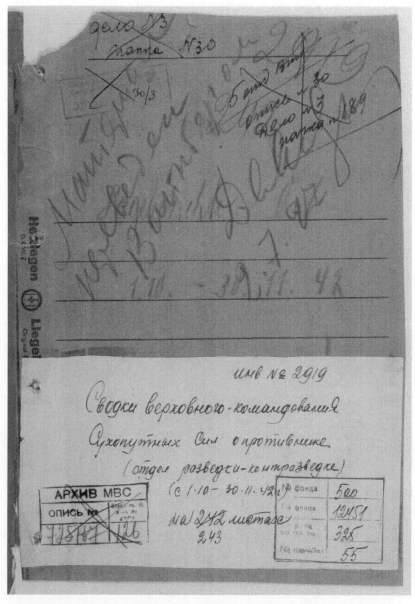

Oberkommando des Heeres, Generalstab des Heeres, Fremde Heere Ost
Army High Command, General Staff, Intel Reports October - November 1942
(Russian translation)

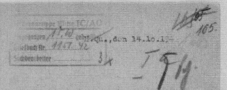

Oberkommando des Heeres
Generalstab des Heeres
Abt.Fremde Heere Ost(I)
　Nr.5058/42 geh.
　　A.

G e h e i m !

L a g e b e r i c h t O s t Nr.488.

A. Heeresgruppe A:
　1.)Gesamtbild:
　　Vor dem rechten Flügel und der Mitte der Angriffsgruppe
Tuapsse verlor der Feind wichtige Höhenstellungen. An den
übrigen Fronten zeigt das Feindbild keine Veränderungen.
　2.)Im Einzelnen:
　　AOK 17: Gruppe Wetzel: Ostw.Mefodjewskij wurde der Feind
durch eigenen Angriff aus mehreren in den Fels gehauenen Kampf-
ständen geworfen. Vor der übrigen Front nur fdl.Spähtrupptätig-
keit.

　　Angriffsgruppe Tuapsse: Hartnäckig kämpfender Gegner wurde
durch eigenen Angriff aus seinen Stellungen und Kampfanlagen
auf dem Höhenkamm nördl. und nordostw.Chatyps sowie aus dem
Ostteil des Ortes geworfen. Gegen erbitterten Feindwiderstand
wurden die Stellungen bei Kurajskaja und Neuginskij durch-
brochen und der Gegner weiter nach Westen zurückgedrängt.
An der Bahnlinie beiderseits Bhf.Pschisch versucht der Feind
den eigenen Vorstoss nach Westen aufzuhalten und durch mehr-
fache Vorstösse das Höhengelände bei Ostrowskaja-Schischel
wiederzugewinnen. Dicht nordostw.Maratuki wurde der Gegner
in seine Ausgangsstellungen zurückgedrängt. Der Feind auf
Höhe 1010 führte am heutigen Tage keine Angriffe. Angriffe des
Gegners gegen Kurdshipskij wurden abgewiesen. Zwischen Kurdshipskij und Tenneleskoje verhindert Feind in unbekannter
Stärke eigenen Entlastungsvorstoss in Richtung des immer noch
eingeschlossenen Tenneleskoje.

Intel report for 14.10.42 1/7 (Army Group A)

Hochgebirgs-Front: Gegen Saantschero- und Allischtrachu-Pass
in Stärke von je 2 Kp. geführte Angriffe wurden unter hohen
Feindverlusten abgeschlagen.

1.Pz.Armee: Bef.-St.Gen.Steinbauer und III.Pz.Korps; Keine
Veränderung der Feindlage.

LII.AK: Bei 111.JD zwischen 2 Kampfgruppen am 12.10. einge-
drungener Gegner wurde geworfen und in Nachstossen eine Höhen-
rippe genommen.

XXXX.Pz.Korps: Feind verhielt sich infanteristisch ruhig.
Eigene Aufklärung stellte unverändert starke Feindbesetzung i.
der Flußschleife südwestl.Jschorskaja fest. Durch kampfkräftige
Aufklärung wurde schwächerer Gegner aus Kalenkoff geworfen.
In der Nordost- und Ostflanke keine Veränderung der Feindlage.

Luftaufklärung: 2o km nordwestl.Terekli Mekteb wurde
erstmalig ein schwachbelegter fdl.Flugplatz festgestellt.

3. Truppenfeststellungen:

   a.) Wieder aufgetreten ist:

      15.Pz.Brig. südostw.Malgobok (23km südl.Mosdok,LII.AK).
      Die letzmalig Ende Juli 42 vor Pz.AOK 1 am
      Manytsch festgestellte Brig. soll bei Baku
      aufgefrischt worden sein und jetzt angeblich
      23 amerk.Pz.haben.

   b.) Einsatzraum hat gewechselt:

      392.Schtz.Div., bisher südl.Nowo Jwanowskij (15 km süd-
      südwestl.Prochladnyj, III.Pz.Korps), jetzt
      mit SR 8o5 bei Gundelen (7o km westsüdwestl.
      Prochladnyj, Bef.St.Gen.Steinbauer). Div.-
      Gefechtsstand angeblich Gundelen.

   c.) Sonstiges:

      Stab Schwarzmeer-Gr.Gr., bisher nordwestl.Tuapsse ange-
      nommen, kann auch ff im ... südostw.
      Tuapsse vermutet werden. (AOK 17).

      IV.Gde.Kav.Korps, bisher in Gegend 5o km nordnordost
      Grosnyj, jetzt nach VII vermutlich im St
      lungswechsel in nordwestl.Richtung.(Pz.AOK

Intel report for 14.10.42 2/7 (1st Panzer Army)

B. Heeresgruppe B:

  1.) Gesamtbild:

    Jn Stalingrad leistete der Gegner gegenüber dem deutschen Angriff zähesten Widerstand; er konnte jedoch erheblichen Geländegewinn (bis zum Traktorenwerk " Dehershinskij ", Stadtplan) nicht verhindern. Die Kämpfe sind noch im Gange.

    Ein schwächerer Fesselungsangriff des Russen zwischen Wolga und Don hatte keinen Erfolg.

    An den übrigen Fronten der Heeresgruppe fanden keine grösseren Kampfhandlungen statt.

  2.) Jm einzelnen:

    4.Pz.Armee: Bei VI.rum.AK. gelang einer schwachen Feind= gruppe nordwestl. Zaza ein örtlicher Einbruch; sie wurde vernichtet. Die Luftaufklärung stellte erneut Ansammlungen und Fährverkehr im Raum um Beketowka fest.

    6.Armee: Jn Stalingrad (Stadtplan) verlor der Gegner das Gelände bis zum Westrand des Traktorenwerkes "Deher= shinskij " und musste einem örtlichen Einbruch in das Werk Raum geben. Nördl. davon verlor er Teile des grossen Häuser= blocks südl. des Gorodischtsche-Baches.

    An der Nordfront wurde vor rechtem Flügel des VIII.AK. ein panzerunterstützter Angriff abgewiesen.

    3.rum.Armee: Erneute Angriffe gegen das Höhengelände nordostw. Kalmykowskij wurden abgewiesen.

    8.itel. und 2.ung.Armee: Feindlage unverändert.

    2.Armee: Jm Raum um Woronesh Ruhe. Vor eigenem örtlichen Angriffsunternehmen zur Verbesserung der HKL wurde der Russe am rechten Flügel des XIII.AK. über den Weg Olchowatka - Skljajewo geworfen. LV.AK.: Am rechten Korpsflügel griff der Feind mehrfach mit starker Artl.-Unterstützung an und erzielte westl. der Strasse Wolowo - Liwny einen örtlichen Einbruch.

  3.) Truppenfeststellungen:

    a) Wiederaufgetreten ist:

      15.Schtz.Div. südostw. Liwny, vor rechtem Flügel LV.AK., letztmalig Mitte Septbr. im gleichen Einsatzraum in Front, seitdem in Armee-Res. vermutet.

    b) Nicht mehr in Front bestätigt wurde:

      134.Schtz.Brig. südostw.Liwny, vor LV.AK. Abschnitt der Brigade wurde von 15.Schtz.Div. übernommen.

                - 4 -

Intel report for 14.10.42 3/7 (Army Group B, 6th Army)

C. Heeresgruppe Mitte:

1.) Gesamtbild:

Ausser zahlreichen örtlichen Bewegungen vor der
Ostfront der Heeresgruppe im ganzen ruhiges Feindverhalten.

2.) Im einzelnen:

2. Pz.-Armee: Bewegungen mehrerer Gruppen vor der
Ostfront und Verkehr von Meldern und bespannten Fahrzeugen
vor Nordfront der Armee.

4. Armee: Ausser Bewegungen vor beiden Flügeln des
LVI. Pz.Korps und vor der Rollbahnfront keine besonderen
Kampfhandlungen.

Bei 3. Pz.-Armee deuten Bewegungen am linken Flügel
des IX. Korps auf örtliche Ablösungen hin.

An der Ostfront der 9. Armee blieb der Verkehr zwischen
Wasusa und Ossuga und westl. der Ossuga rege. Zwischen
Gubzoff und Rshew lebhafte örtl.-Tätigkeit mit Einschiessen
auf verschiedene Punkte.
An der Nordfront ausser lebhaften Artl.-Feuer auf Nordwest-
teil von Rshew und anhaltend starken Bewegungen nördl. und
nordwestl. Rshew zur Front nur geringe Gefechtstätigkeit.
Auf linken Flügel des VI. A.K. und rechten Flügel des XXIII.A.K.
weiterhin lebhafte Bewegungen zur Front.
An der Westfront wurde in Gegend westl. und südwestl. Bjelyj
reger örtlicher Verkehr beobachtet. Nach Überläufer-Aussagen
befinden sich in diesem Raum 5 Artl.-Regter.
Bei XIX. A.K. wurden in der Nacht Angriffe in Btl.-
Stärke auf Shitiki abgewiesen und Bewegungen zur Front östl.
Belish beobachtet.

Befh.H.Geb.Mitte: Keine besonderen Ereignisse.

Intel report for 14.10.42 4/7 (Army Group Centre)

Truppenfeststellungen:

a) Nicht mehr in Front bestätigt:

322. S.D., bisher vor linkem Flügel XXXXI. Pz.-Korps.

b) Sonstiges:

1. Gds.mot.S.D. (vor rechtem Abschnitt XXXXI. Pz.-Korps)
soll nach Überläuf.-Aussagen herausgezogen
und durch die bisher ostw. benachbarte
342. S.D. abgelöst worden.

111. S.D., bisher bei 3o. russ. Armee im Raum Ischow,
nach VM jetzt im Bereich der 61. russ. Armee.
Bestätigung erforderlich.

194. S.D., bisher an Front nordwestl. Suchnoff, soll nach
Überläuferaussagen durch Teil. 164. S.D. (1 Rgt.)
abgelöst und in südl. Richtung abtransportiert
worden sein. Bestätigung erforderlich.
164. S.D. befand sich bisher im Armee-Res. der
31. russ. Armee.

973. S.D., bisher der 31. russ. Armee, nach VM jetzt der
30. russ. Armee unterstellt (Armee-Res.).

1o4.Pz.Br. nach VM wieder im Raum Aurlupowo (7 km nordwestl.
Belyj), bisher im Raum 12 km westl. Belyj.

AOK 22 , bisher vermutlich in Gegend Nelidowo, nach VM
in Filtschinki (22 km nordwestl. Belyj) festgestellt.

Intel report for 14.10.42 5/7 (other troops)

6

D. Heeresgruppe Nord:

1.) Gesamtbild:

Das Feindbild vor der gesamten Front der Heeresgruppe ist auch heute, mit Ausnahme geringer Zunahme der Spähtrupptätigkeit vor der 18. Armee, ruhig.

2.) Im einzelnen:

16. Armee: Vor der Südfront des II. A.K. wurden Stoßtrupps am rechten Flügel der 126. I.D. abgewiesen. An der Nordfront der Bahndammstellung halten die Bewegungen im Raum südostw. Lytschkowo an.

18. Armee: Im Südteil des Wolchoff-Brückenkopfes wurde vor XXVIII. A.K. ein feindl. Stoßtrupp abgewiesen.
Neben vereinzelter Spähtrupptätigkeit gegen die Brückenköpfe Tigoda und Kirischi vor dem XXVIII. A.K. ist erhöhte Wachsamkeit des Feindes und dazu ein vermehrter Funkverkehr der 54. Armee mit ihren im Pogostje-Kessel unterstellten Verbänden bemerkenswert.

Truppenfeststellungen:

a) Nicht mehr in Front bestätigt wurden:

14. Br. in Front 1. Stoßarmee vor II. A.K., AOK 16, Südfront Brückenschlag. Br. wird in A.R. der 1. Stoßarmee angenommen.

83. Pz.Br. in Front 34. Armee vor Ostfront II. A.K., AOK 16 in Gegend Belyj Bor. Br. wird in A.R. der 34. Armee angenommen.

c) Sonstiges:

Folgende bisher in Armee-Res. angenommene Verbände werden, da sie bisher nicht wieder aufgetreten sind, in Heeres-R. angenommen:

Pz.Batl. 1, 161, 470, 482, bisher A.R. 11.Armee, jetzt H.R. Nordwestfront.
Pz.Batl. 85, bisher A.R. 27. Armee, jetzt H.R. Nordwestfront

E. 11. Armee:

1.) Gesamtbild:

An der Gesamtfront blieb das Feindverhalten weiterhin ruhig.

2.) Im einzelnen:

Stärkere erkannte Bewegungen an der Newa-Front des XXVI. A.K. westl. Dubrowka können noch nicht gedeutet werden. Möglicherweise handelt es sich im Zusammenhang mit dem seit

Intel report for 14.10.42 6/7 (Army Group North)

einigen Tagen beobachteten stärkeren Schiffsverkehr mit Auslauf
einer erhöhten Zugbelegung auf den beiden Bahnstrecken vom West-
ufer des Ladoga-Sees in Richtung Leningrad um Ersatzzuführungen
für die im ehemaligen Brückenkopf Dubrowka stark angeschlagenen
Verbände oder um Herbeischaffung von Gerät für erweiterten
Stellungsausbau.

Truppenfeststellungen:

a) Nicht mehr in Front bestätigt wurden:

43. S.D. in Front 55. Armee vor LIV. A.K., AOK 11, südl.
   Kolpino. Div. wird in A.R. der 55. Armee angenommen.

85. S.D. in Front 55. Armee vor LIV. A.K., AOK 11 im Raum um
   Kolpino. Div. wird in A.R. der 55. Armee angenommen.

268. S.D. in Front 55. Armee vor XXVI. A.K., AOK 11, südl.
   Dubrowka. Div. wird in A.R. der 55. Armee angenommen.

123. Pz.Br. in Front 42. Armee vor L.A.K.,AOK 11, nördl.
   Urisk. Br. wird in A.R. der 42. Armee angenommen.

168. S.D. in Front Op.-Gruppe Primorski, AOK 11, im Raum
   12 km südsüdw. Oranienbaum (Oranienbaumer-Kessel)
   Div. wird in A.R. der Op.-Gruppe Primorski angen-
   men.

b) Sonstiges:

Aus dem Vorhandensein von 2 Pz.Br. und einem Pz.Batl. im
Bereich der 55. und 42. Armee ist anzunehmen, daß die beiden
bisher in A.R. der 55. Armee ohne Nummer geführten Panzer-Ver-
bände mit der 123. und 220. Pz.Br. identisch sind. Die in
A.R. der 55. Armee angenommenen Verbände ohne Nummer werden
gestrichen.

Verteiler: I.A.
Stellen des OKW,OKH,OKL,OKM,   gez. Gehlen
   "   "   Gen St d H,   F. d. R.
H.Gr., AOK., Pz.-AOK.

                                    Rittmeister

Intel report for 14.10.42 7/7 (signed Gehlen)

ся с 805 СП у Гунделен /70 км западнее-юго-
западнее Прохладный, перед группой генерала
Штейнбауер/. Командный пункт дивизии вероятно
находится в Гунделен.

в/ Д р о ч е е :

Штаб Черноморской оперативной группы, предполагаемый до
этого северо-западнее Туапсе, по данным агентуры,
предполагается в районе юго-восточнее Туапсе
/17 армия/.

1У гв.кав.корпус до этого находившийся в районе 50 км северо-
северо-восточнее Грозный, по данным агентуры,
предположительно меняет район действий в северо-
западном направлении /1 танков.армия/.

Группа армий Б:

1. Общая обстановка:

В городе Сталинград противник оказывал упорное сопротивление нашим атакующим частям; однако, ему не удалось
предотвратить захвата нами значительной местности /до
тракторного завода им.Дзержинского/. Бои продолжаются.

Слабое сковывающее наступление русских частей между
р.Волгой и р.Дон успеха не имело.

На остальных участках фронта группы армий больших
боевых действий не происходило.

П. Ход боевых действий за сутки.

4 танковая армия. В полосе У1 рум.армейского корпуса
слабой группе противника удалось сделать местный прорыв
северо-западнее Цаца. Группа была уничтожена. Воздушной
разведкой вновь установлено скопление частей и движение
паромов в районе Бекетовка.

Army Group B report for 14.10.42 (Russian translation)

    <u>6 армия</u>. В городе Сталинград противник оставил местность до западной окраины тракторного завода им.Дзержинского. Наши части в некоторых пунктах прорвались в завод. Севернее завода противник оставил часть большого квартала южнее ручей Городище.

    На северном участке фронта армии, перед правым флангом УІ армейского корпуса была отбита атака противника поддержанная танками.

    <u>3 румынская армия</u>. Возобновившиеся атаки на район высот северо-восточнее Калмыковский были отбиты.

    <u>8 итальянская и 2 венгерская армии</u>. Обстановка без изменений.

    <u>2 армия</u>. В районе Вороне спокойно. В результате наших местных атак для улучшения переднего края обороны, на правом фланге ХІІ армейского корпуса русские были отброшены через дорогу Ольховатка-Силяево.

    На правом фланге L V армейского корпуса противник неоднократно атаковал при сильной поддержке артиллерии и вклинился в некоторых пунктах, в нашу оборону западнее дороги Волово-Ливны.

    Ш. <u>Г р у п п и р о в к а</u>:

      а/ <u>Вновь появились</u>:

15 СД - юго-восточнее Ливны, перед правым флангом L V А.К.
           последний раз находилась на фронте в этом же
           районе в конце сентября, затем предполагалась
           в резерве армии.

      б/ <u>Подтверждены вне фронта</u>:

184 стр. бриг. юго-восточнее Ливны, перед L V А.К. Участок бригады был принят 15 СД.

6th Army report for 14.10.42 (Russian translation)

83 стр. бриг$_ы$ по показаниям пленных, бригады отведены

255 стр.бриг$_ад$ в Кабардинка. До этого они действовали вос-

точнее долины р.Абин /25 км восточне$_е$-северо-

восточнее Новороссийск, группа Ветцель/.

Группа армий Б:

1. Общая обстановка

В городе Сталинград, несмотря на упорное сопротивление, противник оставил: кирпичный завод, тракторный завод, берег р.Волга восточнее завода, а также район до Орловка. Наступле-нию наших частей, севернее ручей Орловка, он оказывал упорное сопротивление. На остальных участках фронта группы армий боль-ших боевых действий не происходило.

П. Ход боевых действий за сутки

4 танковая армия. Перед левым флангом 1У армейского кор-пуса пехота и артиллерия противника проявляли большую актив-ность чем в предыдущие дни.

Воздушной разведкой установлено сильное движение частей и действие паромов восточнее Красноармейск и Бекетовка.

6 армия. В районе города Сталинград противник оставил тер-риторию указанную в разделе "общая обстановка". Его попытки переправиться через р.Волга на запад, в зоне орудийного завода, были отбиты огнем нашей артиллерии и авиации. С потерей места восточнее тракторного завода, противник лишился важного пути подвоза с восточного берега р.Волга.

Севернее района Орловка противник вынужден был отойти на Печетка и Рынок.

Перед северным участком фронта береговой полосы между р.Волга и р.Дон атака противника юго-восточнее Котлубань /УШ А.К./ успеха не имела.

Army Group B report for 15.10.42 (Russian translation)

в резерве 18 русской армии.

109 стр.бриг. по дважды подтвержденным данным агентуры, входит в состав 9 русской армии и находится в ее резерве.

9 гв.кав.див. предполагаемая в резерве армии в районе 60 км севернее Грозный, по данным агентуры, действует под Урожайное /115 км северо-северо-восточнее Моздок, 1 танк. армия/.

10 гв кав.див. предполагаемая до этого в районе восточнее Туапсе на укомплектовании, по данным агентуры и показаниям пленных, находится в составе 1У гв.кав.корпуса /северо-западнее Терекли Мектеб, 90 км севернее Грозный, 1 танк.армия/.

Группа армий Б:

1. Общая обстановка:

В городе Сталинград, в результате развивающегося наступления наших частей, после ожесточенного сопротивления, противник оставил половину территории орудийного завода. Западнее Спартаковка /карта 1:100 000, непосредственно севернее Сталинград/ ему не удалось помешать продвижению наших частей на юг до ручей Орловка. Этим продвижением была отрезана группа противника западнее ручей Орловка.

На остальных участках фронта группы армий больших боевых действий не происходило.

П. Ход боевых действий за сутки

4 танковая армия. Обстановка без изменений. У Бекетовка продолжалось действие переправы.

Army Group B report for 16.10.42 (Russian translation)

Dienstgrade und Dienstgradabzeichen der Roten Armee

Militärischer Dienstgrad	Entsprechender Dienstgrad des Politarbeiters	Abzeichen am Kragenspiegel	Militärischer Dienstgrad	Entsprechender Dienstgrad des Politarbeiters	Abzeichen am Kragenspiegel
Marschall	—		Hauptmann	Älterer Politischer Leiter	
Armeegeneral	Armee-Kommissar I. Ranges		Oberleutnant	Politischer Leiter (Politruk)	
Generaloberst	Armee-Kommissar II. Ranges		Leutnant	Jüngerer Politischer Leiter	
Generalleutnant	Korps-Kommissar		Unterleutnant	—	
Generalmajor	Divisions-Kommissar		Starschina (Hauptfeldwebel)	—	
Oberst	Regiments-Kommissar		Älterer Sergeant	—	
Oberstleutnant	Älterer Bataillons-Kommissar		Sergeant	—	
Major	Bataillons-Kommissar		Jüngerer Sergeant	—	
			Gefreiter	—	

German translation of Soviet ranks and insignia

147

QUOTES REFERENCE

All citations and quotes in this Atlas had been translated from Russian by the author.

[1] Чуйков, Василий Иванович: Начало Пути (Военное издательство Министерства Обороны СССР, 1962)

Vasily Chuikov: The beginning of the Road (Military Editions of USSR Ministry of Defense, 1962)

[2] Крылов, Николай Иванович: Сталинградский рубеж (Воениздат, 1979)

Nikolay Krylov: The Stalingrad Frontier (Voenizdat, 1979)

[3] Центральный архив Министерства обороны РФ (ЦАМО)

Russian Ministry of Defense's Central Archives (TsAMO)

[4] Коллектив: Битва за Сталинград (Нижне-Волжское издательство, 1972)

Collective: The Battle for Stalingrad (Nizhne-Volzhskoe, 1972)

[5] Гроссман, Василий Семенович: Военная корреспонденция (Красная звезда, 1942)

Vasily Grossman: War correspondence (official Army newspaper "Red Star", 1942)

SOURCES AND DOCUMENTATION

★ Archives ★

Various materials from Russian Ministry of Defense's Central Archives (TsAMO, Russia)

Reports and schemes for 62nd Army; 2nd, 23rd Tank Corps; 13th, 37th, 39th Guards Divisions; 95th, 112th, 138th, 193th, 284th Rifle Divisions

OKH-Abteilung Fremde Heere Ost, Referat II: Lageberichte zur militärischen Situation an der Ostfront: "Reports for the military situation on the Eastern Front, Oberkommando des Heeres, Army Group B", F.500 OP.12451 D.318, D.325

Various materials from National National Archives and Records Administration (NARA, USA)

Reports and schemes for 6th Army; 4th Panzer Army; 14th, 48th Panzer Corps; 51st Army Corps

★ Books and Press (by publication date) ★

Collective
Военное Издательство НКО «Бой в сталинграде»: "The Fight in Stalingrad"
(Voennoe Izdatelstvo NKO, People's Commissar of Defense, 1944)

Vasily Grossman
Военная корреспонденция «Красная звезда»: "War correspondence"
(Red Army newspaper "Red Star", 1941-1945)

Alexander Werth
The year of Stalingrad
(Hamish Hamilton, 1946)

Andrey Eremenko
Сталинград: "Stalingrad"
(Voenizdat, 1961)

Vasily Chuikov
Начало Пути: "The beginning of the Road"
(Military Editions of USSR Ministry of Defense, 1962)

Georgy Zhukov
Воспоминания и размышления: "Reminiscences and Reflections"
(Novosti, 1969)

Collective
Битва за Сталинград: "The Battle for Stalingrad"
(Nizhne-Volzhskoe izdatelstvo, 1972)

John Erickson
The Road to Stalingrad: Stalin's War with Germany
(Harper & Row, 1975)

Collective
Сталинград, уроки истории: "Stalingrad, History's lessons"
(Progress, 1976)

Collective
Великая Отечественная война: "The Great Patriotic War"
(Knizhnoe izdatelstvo, 1978)

Aleksandr Vasilevsky
Дело всей жизни: "The Case of All My Life"
(Politizdat, 1978)

Nikolay Krylov
Сталинградский рубеж: "The Stalingrad Frontier"
(Voenizdat, 1979)

Nikolay Yakovlev
19 ноября 1942: "November 19, 1942"
(Molodaja Gvardia, 1979)

Aleksey Chuianov
Сталинградский дневник: "Stalingrad Chronicles"
(Volgograd, 1979)

Collective
Великая Отечественная война Советского Союза: "The Great Patriotic War"
(Voenizdat, 1984)

Konstantin Rokossovsky
Солдатский долг: "A Soldier's Duty"
(Voenizdat, 1988)

David Ortenberg
Год 1942: "The year 1942"
(Politizdat, 1988)

Aleksandr Samsonov
Сталинградская битва: "Battle of Stalingrad"
(Nauka, 1989)

Heinrich von Einsiedel
Stalingrad, Memories and Reassessments
(Cassell Military Paperbacks, 1993)

Antony Beevor
Stalingrad, The Fateful Siege
(Penguin Books, 1999)

Richard Overy
Russia's War
(Penguin Books, 1999)

Vladimir Zolotarev
Великая Отечественная война: "The Great Patriotic War"
(Voenizdat, 1999)

Collective
Сталинградская эпопея, материалы НКВД: "NKVD Material on Stalingrad"
(Zvonnitsa, 2000)

Collective
К 60-летию сражения на Волге: "60th Anniversary of the Battle on the Volga"
(Voenizdat, 2002)

Collective
Сталинградская битва, хроника - факты - люди: "Chronicles-facts-men"
(Olma Press, 2002)

Geoffrey Roberts
Victory at Stalingrad, The Battle that changed History
(Longman Publishing, 2002)

Collective

Солдаты XX-го века: "XXth century Soldiers"

(Mezhdunarodnyj biograficheskij fond, 2003)

David Glantz

Colossus Reborn: The Red Army at War, 1941-1943

(University Press of Kansas, 2005)

Chris Bellamy

Absolute War

(Macmillan, 2007)

Michael Jones

Stalingrad, How the Red Army Triumphed

(Pen and Sword Military, 2007)

Aleksey Isaev

За Волгой для нас земли нет: "No land for us beyond the Volga"

(Eksmo, 2008)

Jean Lopez

Stalingrad, La bataille au bord du gouffre: "Stalingrad, the battle at the edge"

(Economica, 2008)

Mikhail Bariatinsky

1942, Сталинград: "1942, Stalingrad"

(Eksmo, 2009)

David Glantz

Armageddon in Stalingrad

(Press of Kansas, 2009)

★ Websites ★

Stalingrad Battle Data
(www.staldata.com) (www.сталинград.net)

World War II Order of Battle
(www.ww2oo.net) ([www. война.net](www.война.net))

The Red Army in World War
(www.armchairgeneral.com/rkkaww2)

Voronezh State University Club "Memory"
(samsv.narod.ru)

Volgograd State Museum
(battle.volgadmin.ru)

National Historical Memorial State Museum
(stalingrad-battle.ru)

Red Army Orders of Battle
(tashv.nm.ru)

XXth century Soldiers
(wwii-soldat.narod.ru)

The Great Patriotic War
(soldat.ru)

WWII Aerial Photos and Maps
(www.wwii-photos-maps.com)

German Documents in Russia
(www.germandocsinrussia.org)

The Generals of WWII
(www.generals.dk)

CREDITS FOR ILLUSTRATIONS

★

Continued in the next volume of the series

Stalingrad Battle Atlas
Part III: November 19 - November 30, 1942

info@staldata.com

2013-2015

Printed in Great Britain
by Amazon